Substance Abuse
in Children and
Adolescents

Developmental Clinical Psychology and Psychiatry Series

Series Editor: Alan E. Kazdin, Yale University

Substance Abuse in Children and Adolescents

Evaluation and Intervention

Steven P. Schinke

Gilbert J. Botvin

Mario A. Orlandi

Volume 22.
Developmental Clinical Psychology and Psychiatry

SAGE PUBLICATIONS
The International Professional Publishers
Newbury Park   London   New Delhi

For information address:

SAGE Publications, Inc.
2455 Teller Road
Newbury Park, California 91320

SAGE Publications Ltd.
6 Bonhill Street
London EC2A 4PU
United Kingdom

SAGE Publications India Pvt. Ltd.
M-32 Market
Greater Kailash I
New Delhi 110 048 India

Printed in the United States of America

Library of Congress Cataloging-in-Publication Data

Schinke, Steven P.
    Substance abuse in children and adolescents : evaluation and
intervention / Steven P. Schinke, Gilbert J. Botvin, Mario A. Orlandi.
        p.   cm. — (Developmental clinical psychology and psychiatry ; 22)
    Includes bibliographical references and index.
    ISBN 0-8039-3748-2 (c). — ISBN 0-8039-3749-0 (pbk)
        1. Children—Substance use.   2. Teenagers—Substance use.
3. Substance abuse—Treatment.   4. Substance—Prevention.
I. Botvin, Gilbert J.   II. Orlandi, Mario A.   III. Title.
IV. Series.
    [DNLM: 1. Substance Abuse—in adolescence.   2. Substance Abuse—in
infancy & childhood.   3. Substance Abuse—therapy.   W1 DE997NC v.
22 / / WM 270 S332s]
RJ506.D78S38   1991
618.92′86—dc20
DNLM/DLC   90-9242
                                                                    CIP

92 93 94 15 14 13 12 11 10 9 8 7 6 5 4 3 2

Sage Production Editor: Diane S. Foster

To Mary—S.P.S.
To my wife, Lisa, and my children, Jamie and Kathryn—G.J.B.
To Marlena—M.A.O.

CONTENTS

SERIES EDITOR'S INTRODUCTION

Interest in child development and adjustment is by no means new. Yet, only recently has the study of children benefited from advances in both clinical and scientific research. Advances in the social and biological sciences, the emergence of disciplines and subdisciplines that focus exclusively on childhood and adolescence, and greater appreciation of the impact of such influences as the family, peers, and school have helped accelerate research on developmental psychopathology. Apart from interest in the study of child development and adjustment for its own sake, the need to address clinical problems of adulthood naturally draws one to investigate precursors in childhood and adolescence.

Within a relatively brief period, the study of psychopathology among children and adolescents has proliferated considerably. Several different professional journals, annual book series, and handbooks devoted entirely to the study of children and adolescents and their adjustment document the proliferation of work in the field. Nevertheless, there is a paucity of resource material that presents information in an authoritative, systematic, and disseminable fashion. There is a need within the field to convey the latest developments and to represent different disciplines, approaches, and conceptual views to the topics of childhood and adolescent adjustment and maladjustment.

The Sage Series *Developmental Clinical Psychology and Psychiatry* is designed to serve uniquely several needs of the field. The series encompasses individual monographs prepared by experts in the fields of clinical child psychology, child psychiatry, child development, and related disciplines. The primary focus is on developmental psychopathology, which here refers broadly to the diagnosis, assessment, treatment, and prevention of problems that arise in the period from infancy through adolescence. A working assumption of the series is that understanding, identifying, and treating problems of youth must draw on multiple disciplines and diverse views within a given discipline.

The task of individual contributors is to present the latest theory and research on various topics, including specific types of dysfunction, diagnostic and treatment approaches, and special problem areas that affect adjustment. Core topics within clinical work are addressed by the series.

Authors are asked to bridge potential theory, research, and clinical practice and to outline the current status and future directions. The goals of the series and the tasks presented to individual contributors are demanding. We have been extremely fortunate in recruiting leaders in the fields who have been able to translate their recognized scholarship and expertise into highly readable works on contemporary topics.

The present book focuses on *Substance Abuse in Children and Adolescents,* a topic of critical clinical and social significance. Steven P. Schinke, Gilbert J. Botvin, and Mario A. Orlandi elaborate the scope of the problem of substance abuse, current theory and research regarding causes and risk factors, and alternative intervention approaches. Both treatment and prevention are detailed to convey current research and program applications. Alternative types of interventions and approaches are detailed broadly from community, school, and media-based interventions to more traditional forms of inpatient and outpatient treatments. Particularly noteworthy in this book is the material on the evaluation of intervention programs and on the dissemination of these programs beyond the confines of research. The authors are uniquely qualified to address the full scope of intervention, evaluation, and dissemination issues. They have contributed seminal research to these areas. Consequently, one should not be surprised at the authoritativeness and scholarship of the text and the authors' sensitivity to diverse research and applied issues.

—Alan E. Kazdin

PREFACE

This book reviews the causes, prevention, and treatment of substance abuse among American children and adolescents. The book devotes particular attention to the design, implementation, and evaluation of intervention programs aimed at reducing the risks of substance abuse among youth. That attention was born of our extensive work in the development and evaluation of preventive interventions for tobacco, alcohol, and drug use. In addition, the book explores the interminable problem of transferring information developed in a research setting to the population at large. That discussion briefly explores the often disparate aims of researchers, clinicians, lay citizens, and policymakers. In so far as we accomplish our major objectives, the book will direct these individuals in efforts to develop prevention and treatment programs.

Much of this book's content comes from our current work in studies to design, test, and disseminate substance-abuse prevention interventions for children and adolescents. These studies are made possible by funding from the William T. Grant Foundation of New York, the Pew Charitable Trusts, and the Kaiser Family Foundation, which are supporting a substance-abuse prevention intervention among Hispanic-American adolescents who live in low-income areas. The New York State Division of Substance Abuse Services (grant nos. C002980 and C002094) is advancing our research in the effects of generic and focused interventions on high-risk students in New York. Also under the auspices of the authors' institutions, the National Institute on Drug Abuse is sponsoring an AIDS Prevention Research Center. Similarly, the National Cancer Institute is supporting a Minority Cancer Research Center established in collaboration with Harlem Hospital Center, Columbia University, American Health Foundation, and Cornell Medical Center. Additionally, the Boys Clubs of America has engaged the authors in an evaluation of Boys and Girls Clubs in public housing projects.

We would like to gratefully acknowledge a number of foundations and state and federal agencies for providing the funding necessary to rigorously evaluate the efficacy of intervention approaches for tobacco-, alcohol-, and drug-abuse prevention under a broad range of conditions and populations: the Smart Family Foundation, the National Cancer

Institute (grant nos. CA 52251, CA 29640, CA 44903, CA 33917, CA 39280, N01-CN-65-65048), the National Institute on Drug Abuse (grant nos. DA 05321, DA 02835), the National Institute of Allergy and Infectious Diseases (grant no. AI 26387), the National Heart, Lung, and Blood Institute (grant nos. HL 44790, HL 33865), the National Institute on Alcohol Abuse and Alcoholism (grant no. ADM 281-90-0007). Without their generous support and sponsorship, the present book would not have been possible.

We also would like to convey our gratitude to Alan Kazdin. Alan has proven to be supportive, responsive, and helpful at every step of our development, writing, and publication of this book. We humbly thank him, greatly admire him, and hope that someday we will grow up to be like him.

Our thinking about substance abuse among children and adolescents is influenced by many like-minded colleagues. We appreciate especially the efforts of the following scientists and scholars: Zili Amsel, Claudia Baquet, Tony Biglan, Richard Evans, Roy Feldman, Tom Glynn, Robert Haggerty, Richard Jessor, Andy Johnson, Coryl Jones, Alfred McAlister, David Murray, Mary Ann Pentz, Cheryl Perry, Herb Severson, Joseph Trimble, and Ernst Wynder.

We reserve our final and most special thanks for Catherine Bowman—poet, author, and editor extraordinaire. Every book has someone who is really responsible for its production; for this book, she is. Without Cathy's steadfast and tireless organizational efforts when we could not find our way, stubborn perseverance when we needed to make our deadlines, and elegant prose when we scrambled our language and ideas, the book never would have come to fruition. Cathy has earned our respect and praise through her insights, hard work, and patience.

AN OVERVIEW OF THIS BOOK

In Chapter 1 we open with a broad examination of the patterns, prevalence, and current trends of substance abuse among adolescents in the United States. In Chapter 2 we will discuss the etiologic factors related to substance abuse. Chapter 3 is an overview and critique of the various prevention interventions efforts. Treatment programs are discussed in Chapter 4. Chapter 5 focuses on the concepts and issues surrounding the evaluation of substance-abuse prevention programs for adolescents. Chapter 6 examines the theoretical and practical concerns involved in disseminating an intervention into society once it has been developed in a research setting.

1

PATTERNS OF SUBSTANCE ABUSE AMONG ADOLESCENTS

INTRODUCTION

The use of illicit substances has increased steadily over the past 25 years. The bulk of that drug use has occurred among American youth. Since the 1960s, experimentation with tobacco, alcohol, or drugs has become part of the normal rite of passage for many American teenagers. Unfortunately, experimentation with most psychoactive substances all too often eventuates in regular patterns of use, characterized by both psychological and physical dependence.

DEVELOPMENTAL COURSE

Substance use, particularly in its early stages, generally occurs within the context of social situations. A number of researchers have hypothesized that substance use may serve as a major focal point for social interaction and may provide individuals with a sense of group identity (Becker, 1967; Jessor, 1976). Though many individuals may discontinue substance use after a relatively brief period of experimentation, for some the initial period of use eventually results in the development of both psychological and physiological dependence. As substance use increases in both frequency and amount, individuals also begin using these substances in a more solitary fashion. For these individuals, the progression may lead to the use of depressants, stimulants, and hallucinogens.

PREVENTION AS SOLUTION

A variety of intervention approaches have been developed and tested to reduce substance use among adolescents. Unfortunately, the treatment of substance-abuse problems has proven to be both difficult and expensive. Even the most effective treatment modalities typically produce only modest results, and treatment gains are often lost due to high rates of recidivism. Therapists are confronted by a disorder that more often than not proves to be refractory to change, by patients whose knowledge of drugs may be daunting to even the most experienced practitioner, and by a pathogenic environment that does its best to undermine any progress made by the patient through the ubiquity of drugs and a social network promoting drug use.

Understandably, therefore, the prospect of developing a preventive approach to substance abuse is extremely appealing. Yet, the development of effective prevention strategies has proven to be far more difficult than was initially imagined. School-based tobacco-, alcohol-, and drug-education programs, as well as public-information programs, have sought to deter substance use by increasing adolescents' awareness of the adverse consequences of using these substances. Though such strategies have proliferated for more than two decades, results indicate quite clearly that these approaches are not effective.

Currently, researchers are looking to prevention interventions that reduce susceptibility or vulnerability to the various environmental factors promoting substance use and that weaken intrapsychic motivations to engage in substance use. These strategies for decreasing susceptibility to environmental influences involve the teaching of specific skills designed to resist various types of social influences to smoke, drink, or use drugs. Adolescents learn to resist both peer pressure and the persuasive appeals from advertisers. In these interventions, susceptibility to negative environmental influences is reduced further by increasing self-esteem, self-confidence, self-satisfaction, and assertiveness.

EPIDEMIOLOGY

Before attempting to solve a social problem, it is necessary to understand both how many people are affected and the causes of the problem. Below we shall discuss the epidemiology of substance use (i.e., its distribution and causes) before going on in Chapter 2 to provide a conceptual framework for understanding the existing evidence concerning the factors promoting and sustaining the use of tobacco, alcohol, and other drugs.

The proportion of a population having a disease at any given point in time is referred to as its *prevalence* or *prevalence rate* (expressed as a percentage). Although it is important to know the prevalence, it is also necessary to examine *trends* (changes in prevalence rates over time) in order to determine whether the problem is augmenting or abating.

The High School Seniors Survey

A major source of data concerning substance-use prevalence and current trends among American adolescents is the High School Seniors Survey (Johnston, O'Malley, & Bachman, 1989), an annual assessment of substance use conducted by the University of Michigan for the National Institute on Drug Abuse. In addition to the approximately 16,000 high school seniors surveyed each year, recent surveys also have included some data on college students and young adults. For example, the 1986 survey contained data from a total of 15,713 students from 129 schools.

The prevalence data derived from this survey may actually underestimate the magnitude of the problem of substance use because they do not include dropouts (an estimated 15% to 20% of students in this age group), who tend to be at high risk for substance use.

Prevalence of Substance Use

In 1985, the results of this survey found that use of 16 types of drugs slightly increased in the class of 1985, compared with that of 1984 (Johnston, O'Malley, & Bachman, 1989). Cocaine use showed the most significant increase.

Figure 1.1 presents data from the class of 1986. This figure is particularly informative because it provides the lifetime prevalence, annual prevalence, and 30-day prevalence rates of these substances. The three most widely used substances are alcohol (91%), cigarettes (68%), and marijuana (51%), respectively. In terms of more regular use, 65% of the students reported drinking in the past month, 30% smoking cigarettes, and 23% smoking marijuana. Stimulants (23%), inhalants (20%), and cocaine (17%) are the next most widely used. In general, substance use is the highest in the Northeast and the West and lowest in the South. Similarly,

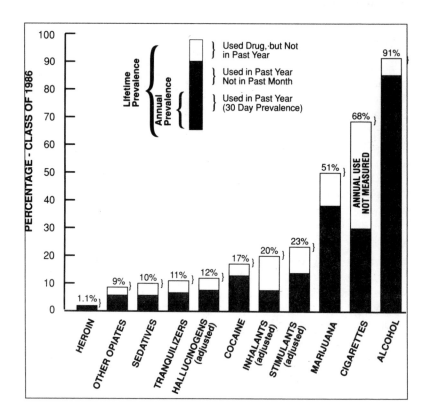

Figure 1.1. Prevalence and Recency of Use
Eleven Types of Drugs, Class of 1986

NOTES: The bracket near the top of a bar indicates the lower and upper limits of the 95% confidence interval.

illicit drug use is the highest in large metropolitan areas (48%) and lowest in nonmetropolitan areas (40%).

Despite the increased concern over drug abuse in the United States, it is important to recognize that fewer than 1% of high school seniors reported daily use of any illicit drug other than marijuana, including "crack" and other forms of cocaine, which when combined, only reach 0.4%. Still, as Johnston, O'Malley, and Bachman (1989) point out, this is not inconsequential, since 1% of high school seniors represents approximately 30,000 individuals.

Substance Use Trends

The existing evidence indicates that the use of most substances has been trending downward since the early 1980s (see Tables 1.1-1.4). Perhaps the most dramatic example is marijuana use, which peaked in 1978 and 1979 and then began a progressive decline.

The use of inhalants and cocaine increased during the same period. Most of the rise in lifetime prevalence of drugs other than marijuana was due to the increased popularity of cocaine between 1976 and 1979 and the increase in stimulant use between 1979 and 1982.

The declines in illicit drug use noted above, however, are largely the result of the drop in marijuana and amphetamine use; if these are excluded, it becomes clear that the use of illicit drugs did not decline overall in 1985 and 1986. In fact, the use of cocaine and inhalants actually increased.

SUMMARY

The use of sedatives, tranquilizers, opiates, and hallucinogens has declined in recent years. Prevalence rates for sedatives have decreased since 1975. Heroin and other opiate use has dropped, as has the use of hallucinogens. Both alcohol use and cigarette smoking generally have declined, according to the High School Seniors data. Thus, though the overall prevalence of illicit drug use generally has not changed substantially in recent years, the pattern of drug use has changed markedly.

Table 1.1 Trends in Lifetime Prevalence of Sixteen Types of Drugs

							Percent ever used						
	Class of 1975	Class of 1976	Class of 1977	Class of 1978	Class of 1979	Class of 1980	Class of 1981	Class of 1982	Class of 1983	Class of 1984	Class of 1985	Class of 1986	'85-'86 change
Approximate N =	(9400)	(15400)	(17100)	(17800)	(15500)	(15900)	(17500)	(17700)	(16300)	(15900)	(16000)	(15200)	
Marijuana/Hashish	47.3	52.8	56.4	59.2	60.4	60.3	59.5	58.7	57.0	54.9	54.2	50.9	-3.3ss
Inhalants[a]	NA	10.3	11.1	12.0	12.7	11.9	12.3	12.8	13.6	14.4	15.4	15.9	+0.5
Inhalants Adjusted[b]	NA	NA	NA	NA	18.2	17.3	17.2	17.7	18.2	18.0	18.1	20.1	+2.0s
Amyl & Butyl Nitrites[c]	NA	NA	NA	NA	11.1	11.1	10.1	9.8	8.4	8.1	7.9	8.6	+0.7
Hallucinogens	16.3	15.1	13.9	14.3	14.1	13.3	13.3	12.5	11.9	10.7	10.3	9.7	-0.6
Hallucinogens Adjusted[d]	NA	NA	NA	NA	17.7	15.6	15.3	14.3	13.6	12.3	12.1	11.9	-0.2
LSD	11.3	11.0	9.8	9.7	9.5	9.3	9.8	9.6	8.9	8.0	7.5	7.2	-0.3
PCP[c]	NA	NA	NA	NA	12.8	9.6	7.8	6.0	5.6	5.0	4.9	4.8	-0.1
Cocaine	9.0	9.7	10.8	12.9	15.4	15.7	16.5	16.0	16.2	16.1	17.3	16.9	-0.4
Heroin	2.2	1.8	1.8	1.6	1.1	1.1	1.1	1.2	1.2	1.3	1.2	1.1	-0.1
Other opiates[e]	9.0	9.6	10.3	9.9	10.1	9.8	10.1	9.6	9.4	9.7	10.2	9.0	-1.2s
Stimulants[e]	22.3	22.6	23.0	22.9	24.2	26.4	32.2	35.6	35.4	NA	NA	NA	NA
Stimulants Adjusted[e,f]	NA	NA	NA	NA	NA	NA	NA	27.9	26.9	27.9	26.2	23.4	-2.8ss
Sedatives[e]	18.2	17.7	17.4	16.0	14.6	14.9	16.0	15.2	14.4	13.3	11.8	10.4	-1.4s
Barbiturates[e]	16.9	16.2	15.6	13.7	11.8	11.0	11.3	10.3	9.9	9.9	9.2	8.4	-0.8
Methaqualone[e]	8.1	7.8	8.5	7.9	8.3	9.5	10.6	10.7	10.1	8.3	6.7	5.2	-1.5ss
Tranquilizers[e]	17.0	16.8	18.0	17.0	16.3	15.2	14.7	14.0	13.3	12.4	11.9	10.9	-1.0
Alcohol	90.4	91.9	92.5	93.1	93.0	93.2	92.6	92.8	92.6	92.6	92.2	91.3	-0.9
Cigarettes	73.6	75.4	75.7	75.3	75.0	71.0	71.0	70.1	70.6	69.7	68.8	67.6	-1.2

NOTES: Level of significance of differences between the two most recent classes: s = .05, ss = 0.1, sss = .001. NA indicates data not available.

[a] Data based on four questionnaire forms. N is four-fifths of N indicated.

[b] Adjusted for underreporting of amyl and butyl nitrites. See text for details.

[c] Data based on a single questionnaire form. N is one-fifth of N indicated.

[d] Adjusted for underreporting of PCP. See text for details.

[e] Only drug use that was not under a doctor's orders is included here.

[f] Based on the data from the revised question, which attempts to exclude the inappropriate reporting of nonprescription stimulants.

6

Table 1.2 Trends in Annual Prevalence of Seventeen Types of Drugs

						Percent who used in last twelve months							
	Class of 1975	Class of 1976	Class of 1977	Class of 1978	Class of 1979	Class of 1980	Class of 1981	Class of 1982	Class of 1983	Class of 1984	Class of 1985	Class of 1986	'85-'86 change
Approximate N =	(9400)	(15400)	(17100)	(17800)	(15500)	(15900)	(17500)	(17700)	(16300)	(15900)	(16000)	(15200)	
Marijuana/Hashish	40.0	44.5	47.6	50.2	50.8	48.8	46.1	44.3	42.3	40.0	40.6	38.8	-1.8
Inhalants[a]	NA	3.0	3.7	4.1	5.4	4.6	4.1	4.5	4.3	5.1	5.7	6.1	+0.4
Inhalants Adjusted[b]	NA	NA	NA	NA	8.9	7.9	6.1	6.6	6.2	7.2	7.5	8.9	+1.4s
Amyl & Butyl Nitrites[c]	NA	NA	NA	NA	6.5	5.7	3.7	3.6	3.6	4.0	4.0	4.7	+0.7
Hallucinogens	11.2	9.4	8.8	9.6	9.9	9.3	9.0	8.1	7.3	6.5	6.3	6.0	-0.3
Hallucinogens Adjusted[d]	NA	NA	NA	NA	11.8	10.4	10.1	9.0	8.3	7.3	7.6	7.6	0.0
LSD	7.2	6.4	5.5	6.3	6.6	6.5	6.5	6.1	5.4	4.7	4.4	4.5	+0.1
PCP[c]	NA	NA	NA	NA	7.0	4.4	3.2	2.2	2.6	2.3	2.9	2.4	-0.5
Cocaine	5.6	6.0	7.2	9.0	12.0	12.3	12.4	11.5	11.4	11.6	13.1	12.7	-0.4
"Crack"[c]	NA	NA	NA	NA	NA	NA	NA	NA	NA	NA	NA	4.1	NA
Heroin	1.0	0.8	0.8	0.8	0.5	0.5	0.5	0.6	0.6	0.5	0.6	0.5	-0.1
Other opiates[e]	5.7	5.7	6.4	6.0	6.2	6.3	5.9	5.3	5.1	5.2	5.9	5.2	-0.7s
Stimulants[e]	16.2	15.8	16.3	17.1	18.3	20.8	26.0	26.1	24.6	NA	NA	NA	NA
Stimulants Adjusted[e,f]	NA	NA	NA	NA	NA	NA	NA	20.3	17.9	17.7	15.8	13.4	-2.4sss
Sedatives[e]	11.7	10.7	10.8	9.9	9.9	10.3	10.5	9.1	7.9	6.6	5.8	5.2	-0.6
Barbiturates[e]	10.7	9.6	9.3	8.1	7.5	6.8	6.6	5.5	5.2	4.9	4.6	4.2	-0.4
Methaqualone[e]	5.1	4.7	5.2	4.9	5.9	7.2	7.6	6.8	5.4	3.8	2.8	2.1	-0.7s
Tranquilizers[e]	10.6	10.3	10.8	9.9	9.6	8.7	8.0	7.0	6.9	6.1	6.1	5.8	-0.3
Alcohol	84.8	85.7	87.0	87.7	88.1	87.9	87.0	86.8	87.3	86.0	85.6	84.5	-1.1
Cigarettes	NA	NA	NA	NA	NA	NA	NA	NA	NA	NA	NA	NA	NA

NOTES: Level of significance of differences between the two most recent classes: s = .05, ss = 0.1, sss = .001. NA indicates data not available.

[a] Data based on four questionnaire forms. N is four-fifths of N indicated.

[b] Adjusted for underreporting of amyl and butyl nitrites. See text for details.

[c] Data based on a single questionnaire form. N is one-fifth of N indicated.

[d] Adjusted for underreporting of PCP. See text for details.

[e] Only drug use that was not under a doctor's orders is included here.

[f] Based on the data from the revised question, which attempts to exclude the inappropriate reporting of nonprescription stimulants.

Table 1.3 Trends in Thirty-Day Prevalence of Sixteen Types of Drugs

							Percent who used in last thirty days						
	Class of 1975	Class of 1976	Class of 1977	Class of 1978	Class of 1979	Class of 1980	Class of 1981	Class of 1982	Class of 1983	Class of 1984	Class of 1985	Class of 1986	'85–'86 change
Approximate N =	(9400)	(15400)	(17100)	(17800)	(15500)	(15900)	(17500)	(17700)	(16300)	(15900)	(16000)	(15200)	
Marijuana/Hashish[a]	27.1	32.2	35.4	37.1	36.5	33.7	31.6	28.5	27.0	25.2	25.7	23.4	−2.3s
Inhalants[a]	NA	0.9	1.3	1.5	1.7	1.4	1.5	1.5	1.7	1.9	2.2	2.5	+0.3
Inhalants Adjusted[b]	NA	NA	NA	NA	3.2	2.7	2.5	2.5	2.5	2.6	3.0	3.2	+0.2
Amyl & Butyl Nitrites[c]	NA	NA	NA	NA	2.4	1.8	1.4	1.1	1.4	1.4	1.6	1.3	−0.3
Hallucinogens	4.7	3.4	4.1	3.9	4.0	3.7	3.7	3.4	2.8	2.6	2.5	2.5	0.0
Hallucinogens Adjusted[d]	NA	NA	NA	NA	5.3	4.4	4.5	4.1	3.5	3.2	3.8	3.5	−0.3
LSD	2.3	1.9	2.1	2.1	2.4	2.3	2.5	2.4	1.9	1.5	1.6	1.7	+0.1
PCP[c]	NA	NA	NA	NA	2.4	1.4	1.4	1.0	1.3	1.0	1.6	1.3	−0.3
Cocaine	1.9	2.0	2.9	3.9	5.7	5.2	5.8	5.0	4.9	5.8	6.7	6.2	−0.5
Heroin	0.4	0.2	0.3	0.3	0.2	0.2	0.2	0.2	0.2	0.3	0.3	0.2	−0.1
Other opiates[e]	2.1	2.0	2.8	2.1	2.4	2.4	2.1	1.8	1.8	1.8	2.3	2.0	−0.3
Stimulants[e]	8.5	7.7	8.8	8.7	9.9	12.1	15.8	13.7	12.4	NA	NA	NA	NA
Stimulants Adjusted[e,f]	NA	NA	NA	NA	NA	NA	NA	10.7	8.9	8.3	6.8	5.5	−1.3ss
Sedatives[e]	5.4	4.5	5.1	4.2	4.4	4.8	4.6	3.4	3.0	2.3	2.4	2.2	−0.2
Barbiturates[e]	4.7	3.9	4.3	3.2	3.2	2.9	2.6	2.0	2.1	1.7	2.0	1.8	−0.2
Methaqualone[e]	2.1	1.6	2.3	1.9	2.3	3.3	3.1	2.4	1.8	1.1	1.0	0.8	−0.2
Tranquilizers[e]	4.1	4.0	4.6	3.4	3.7	3.1	2.7	2.4	2.5	2.1	2.1	2.1	0.0
Alcohol	68.2	68.3	71.2	72.1	71.8	72.0	70.7	69.7	69.4	67.2	65.9	65.3	−0.6
Cigarettes	36.7	38.8	38.4	36.7	34.4	30.5	29.4	30.0	30.3	29.3	30.1	29.6	−0.5

NOTES: Level of significance of differences between the two most recent classes: s = .05, ss = 0.1, sss = .001. NA indicates data not available.
[a] Data based on four questionnaire forms. N is four-fifths of N indicated.
[b] Adjusted for underreporting of amyl and butyl nitrites. See text for details.
[c] Data based on a single questionnaire form. N is one-fifth of N indicated.
[d] Adjusted for underreporting of PCP. See text for details.
[e] Only drug use that was not under a doctor's orders is included here.
[f] Based on the data from the revised question, which attempts to exclude the inappropriate reporting of nonprescription stimulants.

Table 1.4 Trends in Thirty-Day Prevalence of *Daily* Use of Sixteen Types of Drugs

	Class of 1975	Class of 1976	Class of 1977	Class of 1978	Class of 1979	Class of 1980	Class of 1981	Class of 1982	Class of 1983	Class of 1984	Class of 1985	Class of 1986	'85-'86 change
								Percent who used daily in last thirty days						
Approximate N =	(9400)	(15400)	(17100)	(17800)	(15500)	(15900)	(17500)	(17700)	(16300)	(15900)	(16000)	(15200)	
Marijuana/Hashish	6.0	8.2	9.1	10.7	10.3	9.1	7.0	6.3	5.5	5.0	4.9	4.0	-0.9s
Inhalants[a]	NA	0.0	0.0	0.1	0.0	0.1	0.1	0.1	0.1	0.2	0.2	0.2	0.0
Inhalants Adjusted[b]	*NA*	*NA*	*NA*	*NA*	*0.1*	*0.2*	*0.2*	*0.2*	*0.2*	*0.2*	*0.4*	*0.4*	*0.0*
Amyl & Butyl Nitrites[c]	*NA*	*NA*	*NA*	*NA*	*0.0*	*0.1*	*0.1*	*0.0*	*0.2*	*0.1*	*0.3*	*0.5*	*+0.2*
Hallucinogens	0.1	0.1	0.1	0.1	0.1	0.1	0.1	0.1	0.1	0.1	0.1	0.1	0.0
Hallucinogens Adjusted[d]	*NA*	*NA*	*NA*	*NA*	*0.2*	*0.2*	*0.1*	*0.2*	*0.2*	*0.2*	*0.3*	*0.3*	*0.0*
LSD	0.0	0.0	0.0	0.0	0.0	0.0	0.1	0.0	0.1	0.1	0.1	0.0	-0.1
PCP[c]	NA	NA	NA	NA	0.1	0.1	0.1	0.1	0.1	0.0	0.3	0.2	+0.1
Cocaine	0.1	0.1	0.1	0.1	0.2	0.2	0.3	0.2	0.2	0.2	0.4	0.4	0.0
Heroin	0.1	0.0	0.0	0.0	0.0	0.0	0.0	0.0	0.1	0.0	0.0	0.0	0.0
Other opiates[e]	0.1	0.1	0.2	0.1	0.0	0.1	0.1	0.1	0.1	0.1	0.1	0.1	0.0
Stimulants[e]	0.5	0.4	0.5	0.5	0.6	0.7	1.2	1.1	1.1	NA	NA	NA	NA
Stimulants Adjusted[e,f]	*NA*	*NA*	*NA*	*NA*	*NA*	*NA*	*NA*	*0.7*	*0.8*	*0.6*	*0.4*	*0.3*	*-0.1*
Sedatives[e]	0.3	0.2	0.2	0.2	0.1	0.2	0.2	0.2	0.2	0.1	0.1	0.1	0.0
Barbiturates[e]	0.1	0.1	0.2	0.1	0.0	0.1	0.1	0.1	0.1	0.0	0.1	0.1	0.0
Methaqualone[e]	0.0	0.0	0.0	0.0	0.0	0.1	0.1	0.1	0.0	0.0	0.0	0.0	0.0
Tranquilizers[e]	0.1	0.2	0.3	0.1	0.1	0.1	0.1	0.1	0.1	0.1	0.0	0.0	0.0
Alcohol	5.7	5.6	6.1	5.7	6.9	6.0	6.0	5.7	5.5	4.8	5.0	4.8	-0.3
Cigarettes	26.9	28.8	28.8	27.5	25.4	21.3	20.3	21.1	21.2	18.7	19.5	18.7	-0.8

NOTES: Level of significance of differences between the two most recent classes: s = .05, ss = 0.1, sss = .001. NA indicates data not available.

[a] Data based on four questionnaire forms. N is four-fifths of N indicated.

[b] Adjusted for underreporting of amyl and butyl nitrites. See text for details.

[c] Data based on a single questionnaire form. N is one-fifth of N indicated.

[d] Adjusted for underreporting of PCP. See text for details.

[e] Only drug use that was not under a doctor's orders is included here.

[f] Based on the data from the revised question, which attempts to exclude the inappropriate reporting of nonprescription stimulants.

2

ETIOLOGY AND THEORY

INTRODUCTION

Considerable research has been conducted over the years in an effort to learn more about the etiology, or causes, of tobacco, alcohol, and drug abuse. Before discussing approaches to substance-use prevention in Chapter 3, some of the factors associated with the causes and origins of substance abuse will be summarized briefly. The summary will help provide a context for understanding existing substance-abuse prevention programs and evaluating the appropriateness of specific prevention strategies.

ETIOLOGIC FACTORS

Much of the early information concerning the antecedents of substance use was based on retrospective studies. These studies attempted to identify a relationship between individuals' current substance-use behavior and other antecedent behaviors, attitudes, or events. Though suggestive, these studies generally have been criticized by reviewers on methodological grounds, partly because they inevitably must rely on memories or records that may be less than accurate.

Information also has been obtained from a number of cross-sectional studies that look at relationships among data which, though collected in the present, are limited to a single point in time and, therefore, are unable to provide clear-cut proof of a causal relationship. Only a limited amount of information concerning the etiology of substance use has been collected from longitudinal studies, which, because they follow individuals over time, provide the strongest evidence of a causal relationship.

The extant literature indicates that the initiation and early stages of substance use are promoted by a complex array of cognitive, psychological, attitudinal, social, personality, pharmacological, and developmental factors, as well as knowledge and normative expectations (e.g., Blum & Richards, 1979; Braucht, Follingstadt, Barkash, & Berry 1973; Jessor, 1976; Meyer & Mirin, 1979; Ray, 1974; Wechsler, 1976).

Developmental. During the adolescent years, individuals typically will experiment with a wide range of behaviors and life-style patterns. This experimentation is all part of the natural process of separating from parents, developing a sense of autonomy and independence, establishing a personal identity, and acquiring the skills necessary for functioning effectively in the adult world. The same developmental processes that are prerequisites for becoming healthy adults may also drive adolescents to risk-taking behavior.

Adolescents who are impatient to assume adult roles and appear more grown-up may engage in these behaviors as a way of laying claim to adult status. On the other hand, both age-graded and illicit behaviors may be engaged in because they provide adolescents with a means of establishing solidarity with a particular group, rebelling against parental authority, or establishing their own identity.

A common characteristic of adolescents that increases their risk of becoming a substance abuser is a sense of immortality and invulnerability. Adolescent substance users exhibit a remarkable absence of concern about the adverse consequences related to their use of psychoactive substances. This sense of invulnerability is particularly evident during the early stages of substance use and may perhaps help explain why adolescents so cavalierly disregard warnings from parents, teachers, and health professionals.

Cognitive. Significant cognitive changes also take place during adolescence. In contrast to the preadolescent's "concrete operational" mode of thinking, which is characteristically rigid, literal, and grounded in the "here and now," adolescent thought is more relative, abstract, and hypothetical (Piaget, 1962). In general, this thought pattern enables adolescents to conceive of a wide range of possibilities and logical alternatives, to accept deviations from established rules, and to recognize the frequently irrational and sometimes inconsistent nature of adult behavior.

These changes in the manner in which adolescents think may serve to undermine previously acquired knowledge relating to the potential risks of smoking, drinking, or using drugs. For example, the "formal operational" thinking of the adolescent facilitates the discovery of inconsistencies or logical flaws in arguments advanced by adults concerning the health risks associated with substance use. Similarly, this new mode of thinking may enable adolescents to formulate counterarguments to anti-drug messages, which may in turn permit rationalizations for ignoring potential risks, particularly if substance use is perceived to have social or personal benefits. In fact, given the priority of social issues for adolescents, it has been argued that the perceived social benefits of engaging in substance use may override health concerns.

Peer Pressure. Part of the natural course of psychosocial development during the adolescent years is the desire for autonomy and independence and a decreased reliance on parents. Parental influence begins to decline during the early childhood years and continues well into adolescence. This decline in parental influence is accompanied by a corresponding increase in the influence of peers (Utech & Hoving, 1969). Peer-group influence may facilitate the promotion of substance use.

Increased dependence on the peer group is accompanied typically by a corresponding rise in conformity behavior. Preschool children are almost totally impervious to conformity pressure (Hartup, 1970), but the tendency to conform to group norms increases during middle childhood (Costanzo & Shaw, 1966). Conformity behavior increases rapidly during preadolescence and early adolescence, and declines steadily from middle to late adolescence (Mussen, Conger, & Kagan, 1974). However, despite this general developmental trend toward conformity, an individual's susceptibility may vary greatly. Furthermore, differential susceptibility to conformity pressure has been shown to be a function of gender and personality characteristics. Girls tend to be more conforming to peer-group pressure than boys (Maccoby & Masters, 1970); individuals who are more dependent and anxious (Walters, Marshall, & Shooter, 1960) and who have low self-esteem and high social sensitivity (Hartup, 1970) tend to be more conforming.

Family. By far, the strongest factors associated with substance use concern both the behavior and the attitudes of the family. Individuals who have family members or friends who are substance users have a significantly increased risk of becoming substance users themselves.

Media. Researchers have paid surprisingly little attention to the popular media, in which substance abuse is often associated with popularity, sophistication, success, sex appeal, and good times. Both the modeling of substance-use behavior by media personalities and the messages communicated are powerful sources of influence that promote and support substance use.

Knowledge, Attitudes, and Expectations. Individuals who are unaware of the adverse consequences and those who have positive attitudes about drugs are more likely to become substance users than those with either greater knowledge or more negative attitudes. Closely related to substance-use attitudes are normative expectations. Individuals who perceive substance use to be widespread and view it as normal behavior are more likely to engage in substance use.

Psychological Characteristics. Substance use has been found to be associated with a variety of psychological characteristics, such as low self-esteem, low self-confidence, low self-satisfaction, a greater need for social approval, high anxiety, low assertiveness, greater rebelliousness, low personal control, low self-efficacy, and an impatience to acquire adult status.

Pharmacological Effects. Tobacco, alcohol, and other commonly abused substances have complex pharmacological effects. Though the pharmacology of these substances varies considerably, virtually all produce highly reinforcing effects. Because many substances produce dependency, individuals who begin using drugs for social reasons may soon find they have lost their ability to control their use. Physical tolerance develops quickly, requiring ever-larger dosages and increased frequency of use. Failure to keep pace with the escalating need for more of the substance produces dysphoric feelings and physical withdrawal symptoms.

Pharmacological factors become increasingly important in reinforcing and maintaining more regular patterns of use (Meyer & Mirin, 1979; Ray, 1974). Consequently, the significance of this shift from an exclusively social pattern of use to a social/solitary one suggests a fundamental change from psychosocial motivations to those tied more directly to the intrinsic pharmacological effects associated with use of particular substances.

Self-Medication. One often-stated reason for using drugs has been referred to in the clinical literature as the "self-medication" hypothesis (Millman & Botvin, 1983). According to this hypothesis, individuals with a specific psychiatric condition (e.g., anxiety, depression) may use particular substances as a way of alleviating the symptoms associated with these conditions. Presumably, during the course of experimentation with a variety of substances, individuals discover that certain substances make them feel better. For example, highly anxious individuals may find that alcohol or other substances with depressant qualities help them feel relaxed, confident, and less anxious.

Behavioral. There is reason to believe that drug use is part of a general syndrome characterized by a particular life-style pattern and value orientation (Jessor, 1982). Individuals who smoke, drink, or use drugs also tend to get lower grades in school, are not generally involved in such adult-sanctioned activities such as sports and clubs, and are also more likely than nonusers to exhibit antisocial patterns of behavior, including lying, stealing, and cheating (Demone, 1973; Jessor, Collins, & Jessor 1972; Wechsler & Thum, 1973).

MULTIVARIATE MODELS

Many theories have been formulated in an effort to explain the etiology of substance abuse. Unfortunately, most of these theories have limited heuristic value for generating strategies that might be effective approaches to prevention.

Examination of the research literature leads to the inescapable conclusion that there is a multitude of interrelated causes with no single factor both a necessary and sufficient condition for the initiation of substance use. Recently, multivariate models have been developed to describe the interrelationships among cognitive, attitudinal, social, personality, and behavioral factors (e.g., Jessor & Jessor, 1977).

Two Theories With Implications for Prevention

Two theories that provide a basis for developing a conceptual framework for developing potentially effective prevention strategies are social-learning theory (Bandura, 1977) and problem-behavior theory (Jessor & Jessor, 1977). The central features of each theory are summarized below.

Social-Learning Theory

According to social-learning theory, individuals learn how to behave through a process of modeling and reinforcement. In other words, individuals assimilate and mirror behaviors by observing the actions of others and the consequences of those actions. Repeated exposure to successful, high-status role models who use substances, whether these role models are figures in the media, peers, or older siblings, is likely to influence adolescents. Similarly, the perception that smoking, drinking, or drug use is standard practice among peers also serves to promote substance use through the establishment of normative beliefs. These influences may suggest to adolescents that substance use is not only socially acceptable but perhaps even necessary if one is to become popular, cool, sexy, grown-up, sophisticated, macho, or tough. This perceived social payoff for substance use is likely to increase adolescents' susceptibility to peer pressure.

Susceptibility or vulnerability to social influences that promote substance use is affected by knowledge, attitudes, and beliefs. Because individuals can establish goals for the future, social-learning theory recognizes the importance of self-regulation and self-control. Individuals who have goals for the future that are inconsistent with substance use and who are aware of the negative consequences of substance use would be expected to be less likely to smoke, drink, or use drugs.

It appears that susceptibility to social influences generally (Bandura, 1977) and social influences promoting substance use in particular (Demone, 1973; Jessor et al., 1972; Wechsler & Thum, 1973) are related to low self-esteem, low self-satisfaction, low self-confidence, greater need for social approval, low sense of personal control, low assertiveness, and impatience to assume adult roles or appear grown-up. Based on this theoretical formulation and existing empirical evidence, some researchers have hypothesized that resistance to social influence could be promoted by fostering the development of characteristics associated with low susceptibility to such influence.

Problem-Behavior Theory

Problem-behavior theory focuses specifically on problems occurring during adolescence, such as substance use, precocious sexual behavior, delinquency, and truancy. The theory derives from a social psychological framework and recognizes the complex interaction of personal factors (cognition, attitudes, beliefs), physiological/genetic factors, and perceived environmental factors (Jessor & Jessor, 1977).

A problem behavior is one that is identified as a problem within the context of a particular value system. The problem typically elicits a social response designed to control it. The social response may be informal and merely involve disapproval. The response may be both formal and substantial, as in the case of incarceration. Many behaviors are age-graded; they are permissible for members of an older age group but viewed as problems for younger individuals (e.g., smoking, drinking, sexual involvement). For these behaviors, age norms may serve as the defining characteristic.

According to problem-behavior theory, the reason adolescents engage in such problem behaviors as substance use and premature sexual initiation is these behaviors help the adolescent achieve personal goals: The behaviors are functional (i.e., they fulfill a need for the adolescent). For example, problem behaviors may serve as a way of coping with failure (real or anticipated), boredom, social anxiety, unhappiness, rejection, social isolation, low self-esteem, or a lack of self-efficacy. These behaviors also may serve as a way of achieving some personal goal: they may, for instance, facilitate admission to a particular peer group.

For adolescents who do not excel academically, the use of psychoactive substances may provide a way of achieving social status. Adolescents may believe that smoking, drinking, or using drugs will enhance their public image by making them look "cool" or by demonstrating independence from authority figures. Adolescents at the greatest risk of becoming substance users are those who perceive that there are no alternative ways of achieving these same goals.

According to problem-behavior theory, vulnerability to engage in substance use is greater for adolescents who have fewer effective coping strategies in their repertoire, fewer skills for handling social situations, and greater anxiety about social situations. For these adolescents, discomfort in interpersonal situations is great, motivating them to take some action in an effort to alleviate that discomfort. At this stage, problem behavior is extremely difficult to prevent unless alternative strategies are available.

One would think that the obvious and immediate way to deter substance use would be to show adolescents that the risks of substance abuse far outweigh the benefits. But unless adolescents are given alternative ways of both coping with anxiety and establishing effective interpersonal relationships, they may be unwilling to forego the perceived benefits of substance use.

SUMMARY

The evidence that different types of problem behaviors are part of a general syndrome or collection of highly associated behaviors suggests that they may share common causes. If prevention programs are sufficiently comprehensive to effectively target these underlying determinants, it may be possible to develop interventions that address several of these behaviors at the same time, obviating the need for developing separate interventions for each specific problem area (Botvin, 1982; Swisher, 1979). This comprehensiveness would not only increase the efficacy of prevention programs but also greatly increase the likelihood of their utilization.

This information has a great deal of significance for the focus and timing of preventive interventions. Interventions targeted at the use of substances at the very beginning of this developmental progression would have the potential of not only preventing the use of a particular gateway substance but also reducing or even eliminating altogether the risk of using other substances farther along the progression. The next chapter reviews various preventive interventions for substance abuse among adolescents.

3

APPROACHES TO SUBSTANCE-ABUSE PREVENTION

INTRODUCTION

Once individuals become physically and/or psychologically dependent on tobacco, alcohol, or drugs, it is extremely difficult for them to achieve abstinence for any sustained period of time. Treatment approaches, which will be discussed in Chapter 4, have been only moderately effective. Consequently, it has become increasingly clear that the most propitious approach to the problem of substance abuse is prevention.

A number of prevention strategies have been formulated and tested. Traditional approaches to tobacco-, alcohol-, and drug-abuse prevention include information education, affective education, and the "alternatives" approach. The most contemporary prevention approaches focus on the psychosocial factors believed to promote substance use. These approaches include psychological inoculation, resistance-skills training, and personal and social-skills training. Both traditional and contemporary prevention approaches generally have taken the form of school curricula. In addition, mass-media and community-based approaches have been developed in order to provide a support for school-based prevention or to independently reduce substance use.

Table 3.1 provides a general overview of traditional and psychosocial approaches. This chapter describes these approaches and reviews their effectiveness.

Table 3.1 Overview of Major Preventive Approaches

Intervention	Focus	Methods
Traditional		
Information Dissemination	Increase knowledge of drugs, consequences of use; promote antidrug use attitudes	Didactic instruction, discussion, audio/video presentations, displays of substances, posters, pamphlets, school assembly programs
Affective Education	Increase self-esteem, responsible decision making, interpersonal growth; generally includes little or no information about drugs	Didactic instruction, discussion, experiential activities, group problem-solving exercises
Alternatives	Increase self-esteem, self-reliance; provide variable alternatives to drug use; reduce boredom and sense of alienation	Organization of youth centers, recreational activities; participation in community service projects; vocational training
Psychosocial		
Resistance Skills	Increase awareness of social influence to smoke, drink, or use drugs; develop skills for resisting substance-use influences; increase knowledge of immediate negative consequences; establish non-substance-use norms	Class discussion; resistance-skills training; behavioral rehearsal; extended practice via behavioral "homework"; use of same age or older peer leaders
Personal and Social Skills Training	Increase decision making, personal behavior change, anxiety reduction, communication, social and assertive skills; application of generic skills to resist substance-use influences	Class discussion; cognitive behavioral-skills training (instruction, demonstration, practice, feedback, reinforcement)

TRADITIONAL APPROACHES

Information Education

Information education is the most common approach to substance-abuse prevention. This approach is structured around factual information concerning the nature, pharmacology, and adverse consequences of tobacco, alcohol, and drug use. These programs are based on the belief that once individuals are aware of the hazards of using tobacco, alcohol, and drugs, they will develop anti-drug attitudes and make a rational and logical decision not to use drugs.

Information-education programs have taken the form of public-information campaigns and school-based programs. Government agencies, community groups, and such voluntary public-health organizations as the American Cancer Society and the National Council on Alcoholism have produced numerous pamphlets, leaflets, posters, and public-service announcements (PSAs). School programs have consisted of drug-education classes, assembly programs featuring guest speakers, and films.

Fear Arousal

In contrast with approaches designed merely to disseminate factual information, some approaches have attempted to dramatize the risks associated with tobacco, alcohol, and drug use. These approaches go a step further than traditional information-dissemination approaches for they provide a clear and unambiguous message that drugs are dangerous and that those individuals foolish enough to use them will suffer grave consequences. A classic example of the fear-arousal approach is the films shown to students prior to prom night, which graphically illustrate the fate of those who drink and drive.

Moral Appeals

Casting substance-abuse prevention efforts in a moral or ethical framework is another approach to the problem. In operational terms, this approach involves lecturing to students about the evils of smoking, drinking, or using drugs. Many early prevention efforts either relied on this approach or combined it with information education and fear arousal. This approach is popular largely because it is simple and straightforward and does not require complicated intervention protocols. This approach has, however, limited effectiveness. Research evidence indicates that individuals who are highly religious are less likely to become substance abusers (Jessor & Jessor, 1977). Still, it is not at all clear that a moral approach is effective for adolescents who are not religious or who do not have the kind of value orientation that would make them responsive to religious or moral appeals.

Affective Education

In the mid-1970s, drug education shifted its focus away from an informational approach and toward an emphasis on personal and social growth. The underlying assumption of this approach is that drug abuse can be prevented through interventions that increase students' abilities to fulfill their basic needs through existing social institutions (Swisher, 1979). Affective education programs typically include experiential class-room activities intended to increase self-esteem, communication skills, values clarification, and decision making. Two noteworthy and widely disseminated examples of affective education programs of this type are the *Here's Looking at You* program (now called *Here's Looking at You 2000*) and the *Me-Me* program. *Here's Looking at You* focuses on building self-esteem, developing interpersonal skills, and learning current facts about alcohol and alcoholism. The *Me-Me* program targets students from kindergarten to grade six and is designed to enhance self-concept, decision-making ability, and drug and alcohol information.

Alternatives

Another approach to drug-abuse prevention that gained popularity in the 1970s offered adolescents activities designed to serve as "alternatives" to drug use. These activities were designed to serve as substitutes for drug use by offering individuals opportunities for challenge, excitement, and personal growth. Several "alternatives" approaches have been developed; few have been evaluated (Swisher & Hu, 1983).

Drug-abuse prevention approaches based on the idea of alternatives have included a variety of recreational, educational, and community-service activities. For example, a number of drug-free youth centers have been established that feature such activities as arts, crafts, music, and sports. Another example is such wilderness programs as *Outward Bound,* which enhance self-esteem and self-confidence, creating a challenge and a chance for youths to experience a "natural high."

Some alternatives approaches attempt to match specific alternatives with an individual's unfulfilled needs. In other words, activities are tailored to the needs of each adolescent. For example, the desire for physical relaxation or more energy might be satisfied by such alternative activities as athletics, exercise, or hiking. The desire for sensory stimulation might be satisfied through music, art, and nature studies.

When considering the possibility of using alternatives as a prevention strategy, Swisher and Hu (1983) advise caution. Although some activities, such as academic, religious, and athletic programs, have been associated with reduced substance use, others, such as entertainment and vocational programs, actually have been found to be associated with increased substance abuse.

Effectiveness of Traditional Approaches

Empirical evidence has indicated consistently the ineffectiveness of traditional approaches to tobacco-, alcohol-, and drug-abuse prevention (Berberian, Gross, Lovejoy, & Paparella, 1976; Braucht et al., 1973; Dorn & Thompson, 1976; Goodstadt, 1974; Kinder, Pape, & Walfish, 1980; Richards, 1969; Schaps, Bartolo, Moskowitz, Palley, & Churgin, 1981; Schaps, Moskowitz, Malvin, & Schaeffer, 1983; Swisher & Hoffman, 1975). Tables 3.2 and 3.3 summarize a representative sample of studies that have tested the effectiveness of traditional approaches.

Researchers have found that programs whose primary strategy was providing factual information are capable of increasing knowledge and changing attitudes toward substance use. However, they do not reduce or prevent substance use. In fact, there is even some evidence that this approach may lead to increased usage, possibly because it may serve to stimulate adolescents' curiosity (Mason, 1973; Swisher, Crawford, Goldstein, & Yura, 1971).

Because fear arousal and moral appeals are used typically in conjunction with informational programs, no evidence exists concerning their independent effects on substance use. However, since virtually all of the evaluation studies conducted with information-dissemination approaches have found no evidence of prevention effects on behavior, it is unlikely that either of these approaches would yield any effects if used independently.

Table 3.2 Studies Testing Informational Approaches

Study	Target and Intervention	Evaluation Design	Results
Degnan (1972)	9th-grade students; 10 weeks	Pre-post	No significant attitude changes
Richardson et al. (1972)	5th-grade students; 10 hours (filmstrips, speakers, discussion)	Pre-post	No significant attitude changes
Weir (1968)	High school students; not clearly described	Repeated administration of questionnaire	Significant attitude changes
Friedman (1973)	7th- and 8th-grade students; 1 class period/week for 14 weeks; illustrations of drug-related situations and decisions	Pre-post questionnaires	Significant attitude changes
O'Rourke & Barr (1974)	High school students; 6-month course using NY state curriculum guide	Posttest only	Significant attitude changes for males only
Mason (1973)	8th- and 12th-grade students; length not reported	Pre-post	Increased knowledge; increased drug curiosity and tendency toward increased usage
Rosenblitt & Nagey (1973)	7th-grade students; 6 45-min. sessions; presented as reasons for use and nonuse	Pre-post; no control group	Increased knowledge; trend toward increased usage of alcohol and tobacco
Stenmark et al. (1977)	College undergraduates and pharmacy students; 2-4 years college-level pharmacy course work	Pre-post	Pharmacy students had more knowledge and more liberal attitudes toward drugs

SOURCE: Adapted from Kinder et al. (1980)

Table 3.3 Studies Testing Affective and Alternative Approaches

Study	Target and Intervention	Evaluation Design	Results
Moskowitz et al. (1982)	3rd-4th graders; 42 sessions over 2 years; Magic Circle technique designed to increase opportunities to communicate in small groups; implemented by teachers	Pre-post (3rd grade); follow-up (1 year)	No difference between those in Magic Circle and controls on variables relating to drug use and variables measuring drug use
Schaps et al. (1984) Moskowitz et al. (1984) Malvin et al. (1985)	4th-6th graders and 7th-9th graders; Effective Classroom Management (ECM) focuses on general teaching style; incorporation of communication and nonpunitive discipline skills with self-esteem enhancement by teacher; implemented by teachers	Pre-post; 1 and 2 year follow-up	No pattern of effects for ECM was observed for either elementary or junior high school students
Moskowitz et al. (1984) Moskowitz et al. (1985)	4th-6th graders; peer tutoring of curriculum in small groups using Jigsaw technique; implemented by teachers and peers	*Year 1:* Pretest (4th & 5th grade) *Year 2:* Pretest (4th grade) Posttest (grades 4-6) *Year 3:* Posttest (grades 5-6)	No effects using Jigsaw technique

Table 3.3 (Continued)

Study	Target and Intervention	Evaluation Design	Results
Malvin et al. (1985)	7th-8th graders; 12-session training by teachers of peer tutors (cross-age peer tutoring); tutors help younger children 4 times per week for a semester	Pretest; 1 and 2 year follow-up	Students liked tutoring but disliked weekly meetings; no effects on such outcome variables as self-esteem and school liking
Malvin et al. (1985)	7th-8th graders; 1 period per day for a semester; students work in a "school store" 2-3 times per week	Pretest; 1 and 2 year follow-up	Students liked daily class sessions and working in store; no effects on such outcome variables as self-esteem and school liking
Schaps et al. (1982) Moskowitz et al. (1984)	7th-8th graders; 12 sessions; decision making, goal setting, assertiveness, advertising, social influences, knowledge of drugs; implemented by teachers	Pre-post; 1 year follow-up	Effects only on 7th grade girls' drug knowledge, perception of poor attitudes; but results disappeared at follow-up. No effects for 8th grade girls or boys

Quite clearly, information-dissemination approaches are inadequate because they are too narrow in their focus and are based on an incomplete understanding of the factors that promote substance use. Even though knowledge about the negative consequences of substance use is important, it is only one of many factors that should be considered when implementing a substance-abuse prevention program for adolescents.

The results of evaluation studies testing the effectiveness of affective education and alternatives approaches have been equally discouraging. Although affective education approaches, in some instances, have been able to demonstrate an impact on one or more of the correlates of substance abuse, they have not been able to impact substance-use behavior. For example, according to a recent review by Kim (1988), the results of studies evaluating the efficacy of *Here's Looking at You* indicated increased alcohol knowledge but no positive impact on drinking behavior. Similarly, an evaluation study of the *Me-Me* program (Kearney & Hines, 1980) conducted with students in grades two through six found an increase in self-esteem, decision making, drug knowledge, and attitudes. Once again, however, no behavioral effects were evident. Reviews of the effectiveness of alternatives programs also have failed to provide evidence that they can prevent or reduce drug use (Schaps et al., 1981; Schaps et al., 1982).

One explanation for the lack of observed effectiveness of the affective education approaches is they utilize inappropriate or untested teaching methods (Botvin, 1984). Although the espoused goals of affective education programs generally include the development of personal or social skills, the methods they typically use to accomplish these goals (e.g., games and experiential exercises) have not been well thought out and appear incapable of working. Current skills-training approaches rely on a combination of instruction, demonstration, behavioral rehearsal, feedback, and reinforcement.

PSYCHOSOCIAL APPROACHES

Unlike traditional approaches, which focus on information education, fear arousal, or moral persuasion, the most promising substance-abuse prevention interventions currently available are those that focus primary attention on the psychological and social (psychosocial) factors. Psychosocial approaches to substance-abuse prevention include components dealing with resistance-skills training, psychological inoculation, and personal and social skills training.

These approaches differ from traditional prevention approaches in several important ways. First, they are based on a more complete understanding of the causes of substance abuse among adolescents. Second, they are based on well-accepted theories of human behavior. Third, they utilize well-tested intervention techniques. And, fourth, evaluation studies testing these approaches have emphasized methodological rigor and have employed increasingly sophisticated research designs (see Chapters 5 and 6).

The initial studies testing these psychosocial approaches were limited to examining their impact on cigarette smoking. This limit occurred because cigarette smoking is the number one preventable cause of mortality and morbidity in the United States, because it is the most widespread form of drug dependence in our society, and because it is one of the first steps in substance-use involvement. More recently, these prevention approaches have been tested for their impact on alcohol and marijuana. Consequently, most of the psychosocial prevention literature at this point deals with cigarette smoking.

An early advocate of psychosocial prevention strategies, Richard Evans's work at the University of Houston triggered a major departure from previous prevention efforts. Evans and his colleagues focused on the social and psychological factors believed to be involved in the initiation of cigarette smoking (Evans, 1976; Evans et al., 1978; Evans, Henderson, Hill, & Raines, 1979). Evans's prevention model was strongly influenced by "psychological inoculation," a concept of persuasive communications theory formulated by McGuire (1964, 1968).

Psychological Inoculation

The concept of psychological inoculation is analogous to that used in medicine. If an individual is expected to encounter the psychosocial analogue of "viruses" (social pressures to adopt health-compromising behavior), "infection" may be prevented by exposing the individual to a weak dose of those "viruses" in a way that facilitates the development of "antibodies" (skills for resisting pressures toward adoption of unhealthy behaviors).

For example, when someone is called "chicken" for refusing an offer to smoke, he or she may be trained to reply: "If I smoke to prove to you that I'm not a chicken, all I'll really be showing is that I'm afraid not to do what you want me to do. I don't want to smoke; therefore, I'm not going to." When adolescents see older youths posturing and acting "tough" by smoking, they are taught to think: "If they were really tough, they wouldn't have to smoke to prove it."

To accomplish this training, Evans developed a series of films designed to increase students' awareness of the common social pressures to smoke and to teach techniques for effectively resisting these pressures. The prevention strategy developed by Evans also included two other important components: student feedback and health information. The student feedback component was designed to correct the misperception that cigarette smoking is a highly normative behavior (i.e., that everyone's doing it), since research has indicated that adolescents typically overestimate the prevalence of smoking, drinking, and the use of drugs (Fishbein, 1977). The rate of student smoking was assessed and publicly announced in each classroom at frequent intervals. In the health-information component, students received health knowledge concerning the *immediate* physiological effects of cigarette smoking.

For this initial study, Evans compared students receiving monitoring/feedback with those receiving monitoring/feedback plus inoculation against a control group (Evans et al., 1978). When the students in the two treatment conditions were combined, their smoking-onset rates (i.e., the percentage of students who began smoking one or more times per month during the interval between the pretest and posttest) were about 50% lower than those observed in the control group. Disappointingly, however, the inoculation intervention did not produce any additional reduction in smoking-onset rates beyond that produced by the monitoring/feedback intervention.

The inoculation procedure may have been less than optimally effective for several reasons. First, students may have viewed the films inattentively. Furthermore, because the films were presented by adults working in concert with school authorities, the films may have had low credibility. Finally, a strategy involving a combination of material communicated by film, followed by class discussions, may be inadequate because it does not provide students with opportunities for the kind of guided practice that is necessary for promoting skills acquisition (Bandura, 1977). Without actual practice, the student participants may have been somewhat reluctant to apply the pressure-resistance tactics demonstrated in the intervention films.

Several variations on the psychological inoculation approach have been tested over the years (e.g., Arkin, Roemhild, Johnson, Luepker, &

Murray, 1981; Hurd et al., 1980; Luepker, Johnson, Murray, & Pechacek, 1983; McAlister, Perry, & Maccoby, 1979; Murray, Johnson, Leupker, Pechacek, & Jacobs, 1980; Perry, Killen, Telch, Slinkard, & Danaher, 1980; Telch, Killen, McAlister, Perry, & Maccoby, 1982). In addition to the differences in the prevention approaches developed and tested by these different research groups, they have two features in common: They all attempted to increase students' awareness of the various social influences to smoke cigarettes, and they emphasized the teaching of specific skills for resisting those influences. A distinctive feature of these approaches, as compared with the approach pioneered by Evans, is that they rely less on psychological inoculation and more on the teaching of social resistance skills.

Resistance-Skills Training

Resistance-skills training stresses the importance of social influences among adolescents. These influences, which come from family, peers, and the mass media, shape the adolescent's perceptions of what constitutes normal, acceptable, or even desirable behavior. As Bandura (1977) has indicated, all human behavior is a product of the interaction between individual histories, the community, and the larger society.

Resistance-skills training approaches generally teach students how to recognize, handle, and avoid situations in which they will have a high likelihood of experiencing peer pressure to smoke, drink, or use drugs. Typically, this training includes teaching students the specific content of a refusal message and how to deliver it in the most effective way. Students role-play and practice these skills in class and after school. Many resistance-skills training programs use peer leaders as program providers, since peers frequently have higher credibility with adolescents than adults have.

As in the case of psychological inoculation approaches, there is an emphasis on combating the perception that substance use is widespread. Finally, these programs typically include a component designed to increase students' awareness of tobacco and alcoholic beverage advertisements and to teach counterarguments to the messages utilized by advertisers.

Below, Table 3.4 describes several studies which have tested the effectiveness of psychosocial approaches.

Considerable research has been conducted and published in recent years documenting the effectiveness of resistance-skills training. These

Table 3.4 Studies Testing Psychosocial Approaches

Study	Target and Intervention	Evaluation Design	Results
Evans et al. (1978)	7th graders; 4-session social pressures curriculum using videotapes, small group discussion, and feedback on smoking rates; peers used in videotapes	Pre-post	Smoking onset rates for initial nonsmokers exposed to the social pressures curriculum did not differ from onset rates for subjects exposed to repeated testing and a film on physiological effects of smoking
Evans et al. (1981)	7th graders with repeat interventions in 8th and 9th grades; same as above	Pre-post; follow-up (2 years)	Less smoking behavior and fewer intentions to smoke for experimental subjects at end of 8th and 9th grades
McAlister et al. (1979)	7th graders; 7-session social pressures curriculum using discussion and role-playing; slightly older peers implemented curriculum	Pre-post; follow-up (2 years)	Experimental group reported substantially less smoking following treatment and 1 year and 2 years thereafter; substantially lower rates of alcohol and marijuana use also were found 1 year following treatment
Perry et al. (1980)	10th graders; 4-session social pressures curriculum that identified pressures to smoke, demonstrated immediate physiological effects, and modeled ways to resist pressures	Pre-post	Proportion of experimental group smoking declined by end of treatment, whereas comparison group smoking did not decline
Perry et al. (1983)	10th graders; 3-session social pressures curriculum; implementation by regular classroom teachers versus college students	Pre-post	Experimental treatment no more effective than two comparison treatments in reducing smoking; no significant differences found between the two types of instructors

Table 3.4 (Continued)

Study	Target and Intervention	Evaluation Design	Results
Minnesota Team (Hurd et al., 1980)	7th graders; 5-session social pressures curriculum; conducted by college students; utilized videotapes, discussion, and role-playing; compared personalized videotapes in which role models were known to students with nonpersonalized videotapes	Pre-post; follow-up (2 years)	Immediately following treatments, personalized and nonpersonalized groups reported significantly lower smoking rates than the no-treatment control groups, with no significant difference between the 2 experimental groups; two years following treatment, smoking rates for personalized group were significantly less than nonpersonalized and control groups, and smoking rates for latter 2 groups did not differ
Minnesota Team (Arkin et al., 1981)	7th graders; 4 experimental conditions included: (a) social pressures curriculum led by professional health educator with media supplement, (b) social pressures led by same-age peers with media supplement, (c) social pressures led by peers without media, and (d) long-term health consequences	Pre-post; follow-up (1 year)	Among initial nonsmokers, the long-term consequences curriculum had most favorable initial results, but 1 year later the peer-led social pressures conditions had lower smoking rates; no differences found for initial smokers
Minnesota Team (Murray et al., 1984)	7th graders; same as above except regular classroom teachers replaced professional health educators	Pre-post; follow-up (1 year)	Among initial nonsmokers, no differences found among the 4 treatment conditions following treatment; smoking rates for all groups combined were lower than comparison group receiving standard health curriculum; differences among groups for initial smokers not significant, although there was a tendency toward higher smoking levels for teacher-led social pressures curriculum

Table 3.4 Studies Testing Psychosocial Approaches (Continued)

Study	Target and Intervention	Evaluation Design	Results
Best et al. (1984)	6th graders; 8-session social influence approach, plus decision making; 2 boosters in 7th grade; 1 booster session in 8th grade; health educators	Pre-post; follow-up (2-1/2 years)	Significant effects on cross-sectional prevalence; significant reductions in experimental smokers; significant impact on "high-risk" students for experimental to regular smoking
Schinke & Gilchrist (1983)	6th graders; 8-session social skills curriculum focusing on problem solving, decision making, and social pressures resistance	Pre-post	Substantially lower smoking rates 6 months following treatment for experimental versus no-treatment control group
Gilchrist & Schinke (1983)	6th graders; 8-session social skills training	Pre-post; follow-up (15 months)	Substantially lower smoking rates 3 and 15 months following treatment for experimental group versus a comparison discussion group and a no-treatment control group
Botvin & Eng (1980); Botvin et al., (1980)	8th-10th graders; 10-session life skills training focusing on communications, decision making, assertion, and social-pressures resistance; adult educational specialists as implementers	Pre-post; follow-up (3 months)	Substantially lower onset rates among initial nonsmokers immediately after and 3 months following treatment compared with no-treatment control group
Botvin & Eng (1982)	7th graders; 12-session life skills training using slightly older peer leaders	Pre-post; follow-up (1 year)	Lower smoking rates among initial nonsmokers immediately after and 1 year following treatment

Table 3.4 (Continued)

Study	Target and Intervention	Evaluation Design	Results
Botvin, Renick, & Baker (1983)	7th graders; 15-session life skills training using regular classroom teachers; comparisons made between intensive (daily session) and prolonged (weekly sessions) format	Pre-post; follow-up (1 year)	Among initial nonsmokers, both experimental groups had lower smoking rates immediately after and 1 year following treatment; no differences found between the 2 scheduling formats immediately following treatment, but smoking rates were lower for intensive format 1 year later; among initial smokers, no differences found
Botvin et al. (1984)	7th graders; 20-session life skills training; implementation by older peers versus classroom teachers	Pre-post	Substantially lower substance-use rates immediately following treatment for peer-led group compared with teacher-led group and no-treatment control group; rates for teacher-led group did not differ from control group
Botvin et al. (1984)	7th graders; 20-session life skills training targeting alcohol misuse using classroom teachers	Pre-post; follow-up (6 months)	Significantly lower rates of use, misuse, and drunkenness at 6 months follow-up compared to no-treatment control group
Botvin et al. (1989)	7th graders; 15-session life skills training using classroom teachers	Pre-post	Experimental smoking among life skills training group significantly lower than no-treatment controls

SOURCE: Adapted from Battjes, 1985

interventions generally are able to reduce the rate of smoking by 35% to 45%. Similar reductions have been reported for alcohol and marijuana use (e.g., McAlister, Perry, Killen, Slinkard, & Maccoby, 1980). In addition, some studies have demonstrated an impact on knowledge (Best et al., 1984) as well as on attitudes, beliefs, and social-resistance skills (Hops et al., in press).

Generally, investigators have not focused on students who may be the most vulnerable to substance use. In one study, however, the prevention program was found to be even more effective for students identified as being at high "social risk" (students whose friends, parents, and siblings smoke) than for other students in the sample, producing an 85% reduction in the proportion of nonsmokers becoming experimental smokers and a 100% reduction in the proportion becoming regular smokers (Best et al., 1984).

Personal and Social-Skills Training

Considerable research also has been conducted to test the efficacy of broader-based personal and social-skills training (Botvin, Baker, Renick, Filazzola, & Botvin, 1984; Botvin et al., 1985; Botvin & Eng, 1980; Botvin, Eng, & Williams, 1980; Botvin, Renick, & Baker, 1983; Gilchrist & Schinke, 1983; Pentz, 1983; Schinke, 1984; Schinke & Blythe, 1981; Schinke & Gilchrist, 1983; Schinke & Gilchrist, 1984a). The intent of these programs is to teach a broad range of general skills for coping with life, in contrast to resistance-skills training, with its problem-specific focus.

These approaches are rooted in social-learning theory (Bandura, 1977) and problem-behavior theory (Jessor & Jessor, 1977). From this perspective, substance abuse is conceptualized as a socially learned and functional behavior, resulting from the interplay of social and personal factors. In other words, substance-use behavior, like other types of behavior, is learned through modeling and reinforcement, which in turn are influenced by such personal factors as cognition, attitudes, and beliefs.

A distinguishing feature of these programs is an emphasis on teaching students an array of personal and social skills useful in a variety of situations that may have little or nothing to do with substance use. For example, these approaches typically include components dealing with (a) general problem-solving and decision-making skills (e.g., brainstorming, systematic decision-making techniques); (b) general cognitive skills for resisting interpersonal or media influences (e.g., identifying persuasive advertising appeals, formulating counterarguments); (c) skills for increasing self-control and self-esteem (e.g., self-instruction, self-reinforcement, goal setting, principles of self-change); (d) adaptive coping strategies for relieving stress and anxiety through the use of cognitive coping skills or behavioral relaxation techniques; (e) general interpersonal skills (e.g., initiating social interactions, complimenting, conversational skills); and (f) general assertive skills (e.g., making requests, saying no, expressing feelings and opinions). These skills generally are taught using a combination of instruction, demonstration, feedback, reinforcement, behavioral rehearsal, and extended practice through behavioral homework assignments.

All of the studies testing approaches to personal and social skills training have demonstrated significant behavioral effects. In general, these studies have demonstrated that generic skills approaches to substance-abuse prevention can produce reductions in experimental smoking ranging from 42% to 75%. Schinke and Gilchrist (1983) reported a 79% reduction in the prevalence of experimental smoking. Data from two studies (Botvin & Eng, 1982; Botvin et al., 1983) demonstrated reductions ranging from 56% to 67% in the proportion of pretest non-smokers becoming regular smokers at the one-year follow-up without additional booster sessions. One study reported an 87% reduction in the initiation of regular smoking for students who participated in the prevention program in grade seven and received additional booster sessions in grade eight (Botvin et al., 1983).

An issue raised by some reviewers (e.g., Flay, 1985a) is that the psychosocial prevention programs that have demonstrated an impact on behavior may merely have an impact on the transition from nonuse to experimental use and may not, in the final analysis, prevent or reduce more regular patterns of use. Evidence does exist, however, indicating that these prevention approaches produce initial reductions in the onset of experimental use, followed later by reductions in regular use (Botvin & Eng, 1982; Botvin et al., 1983; Botvin et al., 1985).

Several of these studies indicate that skills-training approaches, though generally more expensive and time-intensive than resistance-skills training, may actually be more efficient, because they may have an impact on several related behavioral domains at the same time.

Methodological Issues

Despite the emphasis on research design and evaluation that character-izes psychosocial substance-abuse prevention approaches, recent reviews (Biglan & Ary, 1985; Botvin, 1986; Flay, 1985; Glasgow & McCaul, 1985) have identified a number of methodological issues that deserve further consideration by prevention researchers. Many early studies test-ing psychosocial approaches have been criticized for shortcomings in the validity of self-report data, the appropriateness of research designs, the unit of assignment, the unit of analysis, the pretest equivalence of exper-imental groups, and the potential impact of attrition on internal and external validity.

However, recent studies have become progressively more rigorous. For example, recent studies have collected saliva or breath samples prior to collecting self-report data. This procedure (commonly referred to as the "bogus pipeline") has been found to increase self-reports of smok-ing behavior. Other examples of methodological improvements include larger, randomly assigned samples; pretest comparability; and analyses of attrition patterns.

Program Providers

Recent studies have shown that psychosocial approaches to substance-abuse prevention may be implemented effectively by teachers (Botvin et al., 1983), older peer leaders (Botvin & Eng, 1982; Botvin et al., 1984; McAlister et al., 1979; Perry et al., 1980), same-age peer leaders (Hurd et al., 1980; Luepker et al., 1983; Murray et al., 1980), and project staff members (Botvin et al., 1980; Schinke & Gilchrist, 1983).

Most programs rely on classroom teachers to deliver intervention curricula. The obvious advantages of teachers are that they are readily available, are part of the school environment, and have teaching experi-ence. Some programs are implemented by such outside experts as phy-sicians, nurses, and police officers. The rationale behind the use of nonschool personnel is that experts from the community have higher credibility with students.

In the case of research projects, interventions have been implemented by project staff members. These individuals generally have a strong commitment to the goals of the research, are highly trained, and often have prior teaching experience. Another advantage is that project staff members help ensure that the prevention program will be implemented according to the intervention protocol. A disadvantage is that project staff are not a regular part of the school environment. School personnel concerned about "turf" issues may feel defensive; this feeling may be manifested as low cooperation or even may take the form of active efforts to sabotage the project. In addition, once the project is completed, these individuals will no longer be available to implement the program.

Finally, many programs have included peer leaders as either the primary providers or adjuncts to the primary provider. The rationale behind the use of peer leaders is similar to that behind the use of outside experts. Peer leaders have greater credibility with students than do teachers (Arkin et al., 1981; Perry et al., 1980). Peer teaching has become recognized as a highly effective way for stimulating poorly motivated learners (Vriend, 1969), and peer-teaching teams have been used as a way of efficiently providing more traditional health education to large numbers of elementary school children (McRae & Nelson, 1971). Peer counseling also has been successfully applied in several settings (Alwine, 1974; Hamburg & Varenhorst, 1972).

Selecting appropriate peer leaders is critically important. Frequently, the students selected are the ones who are the most popular among the teachers and administration. However, these students tend not to be well-regarded by the high-risk students and, consequently, may actually have rather low credibility. Obviously, it is important that the peer leaders be good role models, (i.e., not smoke, drink, or use drugs).

A method for recruiting peer leaders that has worked well in several studies involves enlisting the assistance of a popular teacher from a nearby school to choose appropriate students. Peer leaders are selected on the basis of their communication skills and rapport with young people who are most at risk. Frequently, the best peer leaders are students who are responsible but somewhat unconventional.

Advantages and disadvantages have been found for using peer leaders. For example, peer leaders do not have experience in teaching and in classroom management (Botvin & Eng, 1982). Moreover, peer-leader programs require considerable effort in terms of training, coordination, and scheduling. This is particularly true for programs in which the peer leaders have primary responsibility for conducting the program. Additionally, the use of older peer leaders (i.e., high school students) may present logistical difficulties if their school is not near the school of the younger students participating in the program. Furthermore, the results of one study suggest that, while boys and girls may be equally affected by social influence programs when conducted by teachers, they may be differentially influenced by peer-led programs—with girls being influenced more by peer-led programs than boys (Fisher, Armstrong, & de Kler, 1983).

A solution to the problem of whom to use as program providers might be to utilize a combination of both teachers and peer leaders. Using this model, teachers would have primary responsibility for implementing the prevention program, thus taking advantage of their teaching experience and classroom-management skills. Peer leaders would assist teachers in program implementation with such specific formal functions as serving as discussion leaders, demonstrating refusal skills, and leading role-plays. In addition, peer leaders could serve an important informal function as positive role models for the kinds of skills and behavior being taught in the program, particularly with respect to resisting substance-use offers.

MASS-MEDIA APPROACHES

It has long been recognized that the media is a powerful influence, shaping attitudes, beliefs, norms, and behavior. Analysis of the entertainment media indicates quite clearly the pervasiveness of drug content in movies, TV and radio shows, magazines, and records (e.g., Winick & Winick, 1976). Magazine ads are replete with cigarette and alcohol advertisements, as well as an ever-expanding array of proprietary drugs. Adolescents watching TV are bombarded with beer and over-the-counter drug commercials.

A number of mass-media campaigns concerning health promotion and substance-abuse prevention have been developed and implemented. These campaigns typically have taken the form of PSAs that run during times of low viewership and rely on information education and fear-arousal strategies.

Effectiveness of Mass-Media Approaches

When evaluated, these campaigns have produced inconsistent effects. Some campaigns have increased knowledge and changed attitudes in the desired direction; others have had no effects; still others have produced negative effects (i.e., have increased substance use). As Flay and Sobel (1983) concluded in their review, "an overwhelming majority of mass-media drug-abuse prevention programs have failed to change behavior" (p. 17). This conclusion is not surprising when one recognizes that most PSA campaigns fail to reach the intended audience.

The one major exception was the counteradvertising campaign mounted against cigarette smoking in the late 1960s, in which there was approximately one counterad for every four or five cigarette ads. It has been said frequently that the effectiveness of that particular PSA campaign was the most important factor in obtaining the cooperation of the tobacco industry concerning the elimination of cigarette ads on TV.

Despite the paucity of research, mass-media campaigns are a potentially powerful weapon in the war against drug abuse. Media interventions, however, must overcome the deficiencies of the past. It is axiomatic that mass-media campaigns must reach their target audience if they are to be effective. Clearly, PSAs should be aired during "prime time" or other high-viewership periods. Furthermore, media campaigns must de-emphasize the use of information dissemination and fear-arousal strategies and place greater emphasis on strategies designed to combat the powerful social influences to smoke, drink, or use drugs. Finally, high-quality evaluation research is needed to develop and refine prevention-oriented mass-media campaigns.

COMMUNITY-BASED APPROACHES

The major emphasis of this chapter has been on school-based prevention and education approaches. Programs targeted at student populations constitute a substantial portion of the prevention efforts initiated nationwide over the past several decades. However, community-based approaches, although difficult to evaluate, offer the potential of providing a supportive context for other prevention efforts.

Parent Groups

A growing force in substance-abuse prevention in recent years is what has come to be called the Parents' Movement. This is essentially a grass-roots movement involving concerned parents from communities throughout the country. The main functions of these groups are to provide support for concerned parents and a mechanism for becoming educated about the problem of drug abuse, to increase the awareness of other parents throughout the community, and to serve as a catalyst for change. One of the best known parent groups is MADD (Mothers Against Drunk Driving).

Many of these local parent groups have come under the umbrella of the National Federation of Parents for Drug-Free Youth (NFP), which was formed in 1980. NFP's principal objective is to assist in the formation and support of local parent and youth groups, now numbering 800 nationwide. The organization sponsors annual national conferences, distributes PSAs, and lobbies state legislatures and the U.S. Congress.

NFP networks with established and new drug-free youth groups. For example, "Reach America" is a leadership-training project designed to help older students educate younger students. NFP also has developed "Project Graduation Celebration," in conjunction with business organizations, to help students safely celebrate high school graduation.

Despite the energy and enthusiasm of NFP members, the organization has encountered difficulties in achieving its stated objectives. A recently completed study conducted by the Office of the Inspector General within the Department of Health and Human Services (April 1986) found that 40% of NFP members were no longer active. Moreover, according to this report, less than one third of youth surveyed reported that their parents were involved. From on-site interviews conducted as part of this study, it appeared that only one or two parents were very active within each local youth program.

Effectiveness of Parent Groups

Although numerous claims have been made in the mass media concerning the effectiveness of parent groups in preventing substance abuse, there has been virtually no effort to evaluate their effectiveness objectively. One exception is a study conducted by Moskowitz (1985), which attempted to evaluate the effects of parent groups on adolescent substance use. In this study, two sites in which parent groups had been active were selected for study. These sites were selected explicitly because assertions had been made that these parent groups were particularly successful in positively influencing adolescent substance abuse.

The parent groups involved at these sites were the Unified Parents of America (UPA) and the Naples Informed Parents (NIP). Considerable information was available concerning these parent groups because a previous study had focused on the organization and development of these groups (Associate Consultants, 1981; Manett, 1983). UPA had been credited with decreasing the use of alcohol and other drugs, truancy, and tardiness, as well as with increasing academic achievement test scores and participation in adult-sanctioned extracurricular activities. NIP also had been credited with contributing to positive changes in substance use and academics.

As part of the study, interviews were developed and administered to parent group leaders and school personnel. Available archival records were examined for student academic achievement, absenteeism, vandalism, discipline problems (including substance use), and course enrollment. Unfortunately, the available archival records were inadequate to document any of the reported changes in student behavior. In addition, school personnel and parent group leaders had different perceptions of the parents' contribution to changes in school policy and student behavior. Moreover, it was impossible to separate potential parent-group effects from other, concurrent community changes that may have been the cause of any observed changes. Thus the task of objectively documenting the presence of any putative changes relating to substance-abuse prevention turned out to be virtually impossible.

Comprehensive Community-Based Prevention

For the most part, communities have continued to rely on substance-abuse prevention approaches that previously have been demonstrated to be ineffective. However, one excellent example of a comprehensive community-based substance abuse prevention program is Project STAR (Students Taught Awareness and Resistance). This ambitious program involves the 15 contiguous communities making up the greater Kansas City metropolitan area.

The project relies on matched funding from a private-sector business, a nonprofit foundation, and a federal agency. The project successfully integrates a community service project with a formal research project (Pentz, Cormack, Flay, Hansen, & Johnson, 1986).

The intervention strategies are based on social-learning theory (Bandura, 1977) and an integrated model of community-organization theory using Rothman's model of community organization (Rothman, Erlich, & Teresa, 1981), Green's system-centered education model (Green, 1985), Rogers's innovation-decision process model (Rogers, 1983), and Watzlawick's model of planned change (Watzlawick, Weakland, & Fisch, 1974).

The core of the program is a school-based curriculum designed to teach resistance skills to middle- and junior-high school students. Over a six-year period, there is a planned expansion from the school-based component to include parent, media, and community-program components that involve community-organization and health-policy interventions. Figure 3.1 provides the community-organization and evaluation strategy, derived from Pentz's (1986) expanded model of community

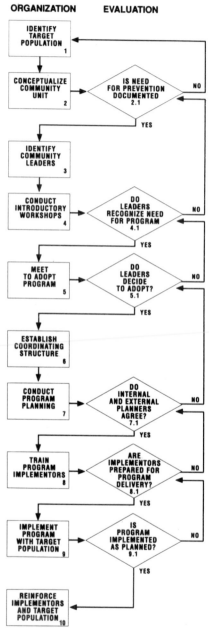

Figure 3.1. Steps to Community Organization and Evaluation
SOURCE: Pentz, 1986. Reprinted by permission.

organization that is being followed in Project STAR. Pentz's model represents an integration of the major theoretical perspectives regarding community organization and provides a practical step-by-step approach that may be followed by those interested in comprehensive community-based prevention.

The intervention is implemented through four channels of program delivery: school, family, media, and community organization. The three levels of intervention based on the principles of social-learning theory are (a) direct training of youth to promote the acquisition of drug-resistance skills, (b) training of teachers, parents, and other program implementors, and (c) ongoing booster sessions for both youth and program implementors.

Thus far this approach has been quite successful on several levels. During the first two years of the project, the school-based component of the program was adopted by 100% of the schools in the Kansas City area and 95% of the teachers. The analysis of data collected in 1986 with 50 participating junior high schools found that the rate of cigarette smoking among the students in the program was 14%, compared with 22% in a control group, and 4% for marijuana use among the program students, compared with 8% in a control group. For alcohol use, only a modest difference was evident, with 10% of the students in the program reporting drinking, compared with 13% in a control group. Ongoing evaluation is currently underway, and the progress of this project will be followed over the next few years.

SUMMARY

In an effort to reduce substance abuse in the United States, a variety of prevention approaches has been developed and tested. When the standard for success is measured in terms of an impact on substance-use behavior, most of these approaches have been found to be ineffective. These include approaches that disseminate factual information about substance use both with and without the use of scare tactics or moral appeals, affective education, and alternatives approaches. As more knowledge has accrued concerning the factors promoting and maintaining substance use, it has become increasingly evident that these prevention approaches are based on incomplete conceptual models that fail to target the most important causal factors.

Despite the failure of traditional prevention models, several promising approaches have been developed and tested in the past decade. Much of the research has been conducted with school-based interventions, but work is also underway to develop comprehensive community-based approaches. The most effective address the psychosocial factors that appear to play the most important roles in promoting substance use.

4

SUBSTANCE-ABUSE TREATMENT PROGRAMS FOR ADOLESCENTS

INTRODUCTION

As discussed in Chapter 3, prevention is the most effective means of deterring substance use among adolescents. When prevention efforts fail, however, often the only available option is a drug-treatment program. There are more treatment programs for adolescents than ever before in the United States, reflecting a plethora of approaches, philosophies, and orientations. Some are run by hospitals, others by churches, and still others by parents. Some are free-standing units, while others are based in psychiatric facilities and other institutions. To date, no accreditation board exists for drug-treatment programs; indeed, anyone with the conviction and wherewithal may establish a center if he or she so desires.

Certain treatment centers are so popular that they have yearlong waiting lists. Much of this newfound popularity is due to the fact that drug dependency is no longer socially taboo. Often parents view treatment as a quick antidote to their children's problems, problems such as mental illness, which may not even be drug-related (Winters & Henley, 1988). Additionally, our society's anxiety over adolescent substance abuse, stimulated by the media and politicians, has brought treatment centers unprecedented recognition.

Even though a definitive treatment approach has yet to be established, most professionals agree that treatment must address not only substance abuse itself but also its underlying causes, such as learning disorders, family tensions, internal conflicts, and behavior associated with puberty (Semlitz & Gold, 1986).

In this chapter, we will discuss treatment-program evaluation, as well as the issues involved in diagnosing and assessing adolescent drug use.

But first, we will review briefly three types of treatment programs: inpatient, outpatient, and residential communities.

OUTPATIENT TREATMENT

Outpatient-treatment programs include counseling centers; halfway houses; educational, vocational, and social service programs; self-help groups; and community centers. These programs may range from telephone hotlines to highly structured therapies involving the whole family. Outpatient treatment is the most frequently utilized type of treatment because it is readily available and inexpensive. The programs vary widely, though most emphasize counseling and do not prescribe medication.

Wheeler and Malmquist (1987) divide outpatient care into four types: drug-abuse counseling, to control or eliminate drug use; aftercare, to support the adolescent returning from an inpatient or residential treatment program; day treatment, a highly structured alternative to inpatient treatment; and family therapy, designed to educate and support the whole family.

Unfortunately, evaluations have found that many outpatient plans have limited effectiveness. Because outpatient treatments do not remove adolescents from their everyday environments, it is difficult for them to recognize and alter their behavior.

Semlitz and Gold (1986, p. 465) have outlined criteria for adolescent candidates for outpatient treatment.

(1) Absence of acute medical and psychiatric problems
(2) Absence of chronic medical problems
(3) Willingness to abstain from mood-altering drugs
(4) Cooperation with random urine screening
(5) Previously successful outpatient treatment.

INPATIENT TREATMENT

Inpatient programs usually are based in hospitals. When an adolescent is admitted to an inpatient program, a battery of assessments is administered, including physical and psychological evaluations, educational and legal status, and chemical-use history. Usually, the inpatient program is highly structured and staffed by medical professionals, drug counselors, recreational therapists, and psychologists (Bailey, 1989). The emphasis is on group therapy and substance-abuse education. The environment is tightly controlled, with daily schedules and strict rules for conduct. Inpatient treatment can be exceptionally expensive. Some daily rates begin at $500.

Most programs are multifaceted, focusing not only on drug treatment but also on such other facets of the adolescent's life as family therapy and educational activities. The length of stay in an inpatient program varies from 20 to 60 days. Most inpatient programs for adolescents are based on such adult-treatment programs as the Minnesota Model for Adult Treatment (Wheeler & Malmquist, 1987). This model recommends a stay of not more than two months, with a focus on the disease concept of substance abuse and a commitment to the Alcoholics Anonymous/ Narcotics Anonymous (AA/NA) 12-step recovery program.

RESIDENTIAL COMMUNITIES

Three main differences distinguish residential communities and inpatient programs. Residential communities treat adolescents who may have serious psychological or social problems in addition to a drug problem. The time spent in treatment is usually six to nine months as opposed to a two-month inpatient treatment. There is also a greater diversity of approaches and philosophies among residential programs than among inpatient-treatment programs.

The objective of most residential communities is not only to change substance-use behavior, but also to develop social skills, assist in education and vocational skills, and build self-esteem and confidence. Most residential communities fall into two camps characterized by two opposing philosophies: that drug addiction is a disease that cannot be cured, and that drug abuse is not a disease but a behavior that can be eliminated. Although these beliefs conflict, both lead to highly structured, intensive treatments involving "total immersion."

Residential communities are strict and strongly regulated, with an AA/NA emphasis. They are known for stressing communication and for openness and encouraging one to take control of one's life. Each day residents attend confrontational encounter groups, individual counseling, and tutoring sessions. They have daily chores and obligations to interact with other residents. The residents progress through a series of stages, each carrying more responsibility and freedom than the previous one. Unlike inpatient programs, residential communities may have only one or two professional staff. Peer counselors, administrators, and role models are often ex-addicts who have been through the program themselves.

THREE TREATMENT PROGRAMS
FOR ADOLESCENTS

MacDonald (1984) reviewed several treatment programs for adolescents. Here we describe three, which exemplify the aforementioned treatment categories.

Outpatient. About 6,000 young people in 14 states attend the Palmer Drug Abuse Program (PDAP) meetings. The organization was founded by Bob Mehehan, an ex-heroin addict and alcoholic. PDAP offers young people and their parents a place to receive help at no charge.

Both parents and children first meet with a PDAP graduate to design a recovery plan. The counselor obtains a commitment from the child to abstain from drugs and alcohol for 30 days and to attend as many meetings as possible. Parents are involved in every stage of the program and may attend meetings to learn how other parents are dealing with drug problems.

PDAP meetings are modeled on the 12-step NA/AA guidelines but also include social events, group "rap" sessions, individual counseling, and "fun time." The only rules are: no drugs, no getting high, no sex, and no violence.

Inpatient. The Drug Abuse Programs of America (DAPA) was founded in 1975 and is based in Pasadena, Texas. A stay at DAPA rarely lasts more than 10 weeks. During the first few days of the program, the youth is examined by psychiatrists and physicians. Staff nurses assess the adolescent's medical and psychosocial history. Based on this information, a detailed and personal treatment plan for the adolescent is designed. Each resident undergoes five hours of group therapy per day, including individual psychiatric and psychological therapy and drug-abuse counseling.

DAPA offers biofeedback, assertiveness training, remedial education, physical medication, and recreational activities. DAPA staff is highly trained, with primary therapists required to have at least a master's degree.

Staff teachers have received special training in working with chemically dependent teens.

Residential Treatment. Young people in Straight Inc. range from 12 to 22 years of age. This intensive five-phase program lasts an average of 18 months. Such terms as *rigorous, marine corps, confrontational,* and *no-nonsense* have been used to describe the program's philosophy.

Residents spend 12 hours, six days per week, in group "rap" sessions. Those in the first phase of the program cannot go anywhere on the grounds without being accompanied by an "old-timer," a peer in Phase 3, 4, or 5. Those in treatment cannot wear jewelry, high heels, makeup, or T-shirts, and they cannot use the phone or talk to members of the opposite sex. The only materials they are permitted to read are the Bible and AA-related literature. Staff members are teens who have graduated successfully from the program and received special courses in counseling.

One unique aspect of Straight Inc. is that during Phase 1 the residents will spend two to three weeks with a foster family. The parents, who nurture, support, and discipline the first-phaser, have a child of their own who is farther along in the treatment plan. To enter Phase 2, the adolescent must show signs of self-improvement, know the program's seven steps to recovery (which are based on AA's 12 steps), and keep a daily morals inventory. In Phase 3, an adolescent returns to school and is allowed to run errands, serve dinner, and accompany first-phasers. In Phase 4, residents are allowed to leave on day passes. By the time they reach Phase 5, they are counseling their peers in Phases 1 through 4. After leaving Straight Inc., they begin a six-month aftercare program.

ASSESSMENT OF TREATMENT PROGRAMS

Surprisingly, few clinical studies have investigated the effectiveness of treatment programs for adolescents. Findings from the studies that exist do not provide evidence that treatment programs prevent substance abuse or that one particular treatment is more effective than another (Allison & Hubbard, 1985).

The evaluator's task is complicated further by the wide variety of techniques, philosophies, and approaches, all of which must be tested before a definitive program may be identified. Unfortunately, most treatment programs do not have the resources or the personnel to carry out rigorous empirical tests. Because standardized assessment tools do not exist, most treatment centers are evaluated informally, using in-house surveys. Consequently, the data describing treatment programs are often idiosyncratic and incomplete.

Comparing Adolescents and Adults

Whether adolescent substance abusers should be treated in the same way as adult substance abusers is a crucial question that has not been resolved (Isralowitz & Singer, 1983). Studies show that adolescent drug users are typically not addicted to opiates and have less physical dependence than adult abusers (Moberg, 1983). The developmental differences between an adult and an adolescent must be taken into account (Wheeler & Malmquist, 1987). Obviously, an adult who skips work to spend the day in a bar can be diagnosed as having a problem with alcohol. But can one make the same assessment when an adolescent skips school to drink beer with his or her friends?

Rather than designing treatment programs especially for the needs of adolescents, most current programs today are imitations of adult substance-abuse treatment programs. The AA/NA recovery plan may be inappropriate for an adolescent whose substance abuse is not a lifelong disease for which abstinence is the only treatment, but a developmental behavior the adolescent probably will outgrow.

Diagnostic Issues

To date, adequate assessment procedures do not exist for describing intermediate levels of chemical dependency among adolescents (Winters & Henly, 1988). Consequently, by the time an adolescent enters a treatment program, he or she is often an advanced drug abuser. The DSM-III criteria are used most commonly to determine whether or not an adolescent should be recommended for a treatment program (Willams, Feibelman, & Moulder, 1989). These criteria include substance-abuse intoxication throughout the day, inability to cut down, repeated efforts to control use, and continuation of use despite physical disorder.

Many professionals feel that earlier detection may help the abuser before severe problems develop. Early detection, however, puts a strain on service providers to make decisions about treatment when there are no psychometric or biomedical indices. Reviewers believe that, besides measuring the level of chemical involvement, assessments are needed to better recognize behaviors disguised by substance use.

SUMMARY

More sophisticated procedures are necessary for health-care professionals, lay people, and families to evaluate levels of chemical dependency and the most appropriate treatment setting for each level (Bailey, 1989). For example, should treatment begin with experimental drug use, or should it be a strategy of last resort for those who are physically addicted?

Studies have shown that younger and less-addicted users will do better in treatment (McLellan, Luborsky, O'Brien, Woody, & Druley, 1982), and earlier detection may help the abuser before severe problems develop. Until treatment programs are designed specifically for adolescents, and until better assessment procedures are developed, adolescents and their families will continue to invest large amounts of time, effort, and expense in programs that prove to be without long-term value.

5

THE EVALUATION OF
INTERVENTIONS

INTRODUCTION

This chapter focuses on the evaluation of substance-abuse interventions for adolescents. First, we present evaluation concepts that are central to empirical research. After reviewing these background issues, we next describe methods and measures commonly utilized to evaluate substance-abuse interventions. Threats to research validity then are examined with guidelines for future studies. Finally, we address data-analysis issues and techniques.

DEFINITIONS

Evaluation research has been defined as "the systematic application of social research procedures in assessing the conceptualization and design, implementation, and utility of social intervention programs" (Rossi & Freeman, 1985, p. 19) and as "a process of applying scientific procedures to accumulate reliable and valid evidence on the manner and extent to which specified activities produce particular effects or outcomes" (Rutman, 1977, p. 16). Evaluation research measures the effects and the outcomes of programs and suggests ways to refine these programs either at the design or the performance stage (Gerhard, 1981; Windsor, Baranowski, Clark, & Cutter, 1984).

Another function of evaluation research is to examine the utility and the worth of interventions. Utility is determined by comparing processes to planned objectives. Worth is determined by comparing processes to held values and principles.

PURPOSES OF EVALUATION

The most frequently stated purposes of evaluations are listed as follows (Windsor et al., 1984):

(1) Determining the rate and level of attainment of program objectives
(2) Planning and making decisions by ascertaining strengths and weaknesses of program elements
(3) Monitoring standards of performance and establishing quality-assurance and control mechanisms
(4) Determining the generalizability of an overall program or program elements to other populations
(5) Contributing to the base of scientific knowledge
(6) Identifying hypotheses for future study
(7) Meeting the demand for public or fiscal accountability
(8) Improving the professional staff's skill in the performance of program planning, implementation, and evaluation activities
(9) Promoting positive public relations and community awareness
(10) Fulfilling grant or contract requirements.

This list suggests that evaluation activities may be undertaken from a variety of perspectives, including those of client or consumer, service provider, funder, legislator or other policymaker, or public-interest group. Similarly, there are numerous evaluation foci, including examining program design, monitoring program implementation, achieving short- or long-term goals and objectives, examining the extended impact of intended and unintended program effects, or calculating the program's relative cost-efficiency or cost-effectiveness.

Even in the domain of scientific evaluation, however, politics are central. Evaluation is always conducted within a political or social context that determines the objectives evaluated, the measures chosen, the types and amounts of data collected, the analytical demands, and the allocation of time, staff, and resources (Chelimsky, 1987).

THREE TYPES OF EVALUATION

Preevaluation

Before discussing three types of evaluation, two "preevaluative" activities of particular importance should be mentioned. *Needs assessment*

(Warheit, Bell, & Schwab, 1977) attempts to determine whether there is a need for a program; *evaluability assessment* (Wholey, 1977) attempts to determine whether the program can be evaluated. These activities are of critical importance in the evaluation process, since their findings may indicate that the substance-use prevention program is neither required nor sufficiently conceptualized to warrant further evaluation effort.

Formative and Process Evaluation

As the name implies, a formative evaluation is carried out in the early stages of an intervention. A formative evaluation may include a pilot study that assesses the short-term impact of the program.

The process evaluation analyzes the organization and design of a program, reporting on procedures and activities, financial resources, organizational structures, program delivery, and relationships between participants and program staff.

Illustrative Example. Perry, Klepp, Halper, Hawkins, & Murray (1986) undertook two prevention projects that utilized peer leaders as program providers. Early in the study, they undertook a process evaluation. Peer leaders were asked to rate the program's activities and effectiveness. These measures were used to evaluate the peer-training component of the program.

Summative or Outcome Evaluation

The summative or outcome evaluation assesses a program over a period of time. Foci of summative evaluations usually include (a) achievement of program objectives; (b) changes in participants' substance-use attitudes and behaviors; (c) changes in secondary indicators of participant substance use, such as academic or work performance and school attendance; (d) examination of program effects, both intended and unintended (such as boomerang effects, in which participants engage in substance-use behaviors to a greater degree than control students); and (e) the examination of specific components of the program (such as a peer role-modeling component).

Illustrative Example. Project ALERT, a school-based prevention program for seventh and eighth graders, targeted the so-called gateway drugs of cigarettes, alcohol, and marijuana (Ellickson & Bell, 1990). This project was based on the social influences model of prevention (see Chapter 3). The evaluation of treatment effectiveness was based on examination of differences in drug-behavior outcomes for students in two treatment groups and a control group at several measurement points.

Impact or Health-Outcome Evaluation

An impact evaluation assesses the effectiveness of a program in meeting its specified objectives with a target population—for example, decreased smoking by adolescents. A health-outcome evaluation assesses changes or improvement in the health status for a specified group of people. Examples of impact and health-outcome evaluations include community-level changes in substance-use trends, prevalence, morbidity, or mortality; changes in substance-use related social norms; and changes in substance-use arrest rates.

Illustrative Example. Pentz et al. (1989) examined the effects of a multi-community substance-use prevention intervention. They measured students' use of several drugs through self-report and biochemical validation. In the impact-evaluation program, effects were estimated, controlling for school-level socioeconomic status, race/ethnicity, urbanicity, and grade.

EVALUATION MODELS

The above evaluations have been implemented using numerous models. The following sampler of evaluation models is an example of what Patton (1981) humorously calls "evaluation alphabet soup" (p. 180).

1. *Objectives-based or goal attainment model.* Programs are evaluated according to previously defined goals and objectives. Strengths: Effectiveness is examined using a yardstick established and agreed to by program developers and staff. Weaknesses: Objectives may not be comprehensive, appropriate, or realistic. Often, this model does not consider related health programs and other influential environmental factors.

2. *Management consultant model.* This evaluation looks at specific problems and organizational deficiencies from a managerial perspective. Strengths: High likelihood of utilization of evaluation results; may employ cost-effectiveness or cost-efficiency methods, which allow programs to be compared using a standard of cost-per-unit. Weaknesses: Perspectives of other constituencies (for instance, community interests) often are

excluded; short-term considerations often are given greater weight than long-term concerns.

3. *Stake-Holder model (Weiss, 1983)*. Incorporates perspectives of relevant constituencies and audiences (individuals and groups involved in the program or concerned with its evaluation). Strengths: Comprehensive, responsive, utilization-focused. Weaknesses: May be difficult to determine or reconcile stake-holder views; may be incompatible with conventional evaluation practices.

4. *Naturalistic evaluation model (Guba, 1987)*. Develops theories and hypotheses based on the views of participants being studied; employs highly detailed and contextualized reports of group and individual actions. Strengths: Concrete, portrays the program in its natural habitat; oriented toward individuals and their experiences. Weaknesses: Unstandardized; difficult to make generalizations; emphasis on process rather than outcomes.

5. *Quasi-Systems model/Context Inputs Process Product (CIPP) model*. These models stress the need to consider context (program circumstances and situations), inputs (characteristics and conditions of people and resources into program system), throughput (processing structures of human and nonhuman resources), and outputs (products of program systems). For example, a CIPP evaluation of an urban drug intervention would consider media attention to the city's drug problem (context), the budget of the program (input), the internal organization of the projects (process or throughput), and the effect of the program's materials and services (product or output). Strengths: Community oriented; multifaceted; considers relationships between various components. Weaknesses: Unstandardized, unconventional, difficult to implement.

6. *Systems model (Dever, Rousseau, & Houser, 1981)*. This model considers all interrelated systems (consumer, organizational, and political systems) and their interaction in examining treatment impacts. Strengths: Widest possible evaluation perspective; takes into consideration disparate influences. Weaknesses: Difficult to obtain and integrate information concerning all relevant systems.

MEASURES AND METHODS

In this section, we discuss and review several measures and methods used when evaluating substance-use prevention programs. We then examine how these measures are used in process, summative, and impact evaluations.

Reliability

Reliability is the degree to which an instrument will produce the same score if repeated. For example, a measure of marijuana use would have low reliability if the measure categorized an individual as a frequent marijuana smoker at one test administration and abstinent at another test administration later the same day. Reliability is a necessary but not sufficient condition for validity (Nunnally 1978). Coefficient *alpha* (a measure of consistency among the items in a measurement scale) may be used to estimate the reliability of any type of multiple-item scale or instrument; it is recommended that reliability estimates using this measure be conducted for all instruments and scales (Nunnally, 1978).

Validity

Validity assessment attempts to answer the question "Can this instrument be used to measure what it is intended to measure?" (Nunnally, 1978, p. 86). There are three major types of validity: predictive validity, content validity, and construct validity.

Predictive Validity. This type of validity is concerned with the ability of one behavior to predict another behavior. For example, Christiansen, Smith, Roehling, and Goldman (1989) compared adolescents' alcohol-use expectancies with their self-reported drinking behavior one year later and found that the two measures were significantly correlated. In other words, the alcohol-use expectancies measure has predictive validity for actual drinking behavior.

Content Validity. The items constituting an instrument must be conveyed clearly and adequately in order to achieve content validity. For example, a comprehensive self-report survey of substance-use behaviors would have limited content validity if it included items concerning the use of amphetamines and barbiturates and excluded items concerning alcohol or tobacco.

Construct Validity. This type of validity is concerned with the degree to which measures are interrelated. The construct represents a hypothesis that a variety of measures will be correlated. For example, social influences theory suggests that children whose parents take drugs are expected to take drugs and to have lower grades. An examination of the statistical associations among these variables would be required in order to test the construct validity of this theory.

Qualitative and Quantitative Data

Qualitative data refers to information measured at the nominal level and generally stored as either narrative text or as numbers representing distinct categories, attributes, or qualities. *Quantitative data* is information measured at the ordinal, interval, or ratio levels of measurement and represents different quantities of an object or its attributes. Early discussions suggested an inherent hierarchy of information, with quantitative measures and methods perceived as superior to qualitative ones. Over the years, however, qualitative measures and methods have become part of the standard research repertoire.

Data Sources

Archival Information. This information may come from government agencies, research institutes, and academic centers. For example, statistical information concerning numbers of residents and household composition, their ages, ethnic identification, socioeconomic status (employment, income, educational attainment), and other useful program-planning information may be obtained from the U.S. Census Bureau and state or municipal health departments. Additionally, reports from private agencies, hospitals, and drug treatment facilities may be highly relevant to the program planner.

One major source of data for process evaluation purposes is the program's own records and reports. These records may indicate the number and type of staff employed on the project as well as information about program recipients.

Survey Methods. Such modern survey research methods as the personal interview, the self-administered questionnaire, and the telephone survey (Bradburn & Sudman, 1979; Dillman, 1978) have proven to be extremely useful evaluation tools. Common survey targets include program staff, participants, administrators, schools, youth centers, and social service agencies. The key informant survey is an efficient but nonscientific method of canvassing opinions of individuals with unique information that would be difficult to obtain otherwise. Key informants could include police officers stationed in the program locale, program alumni, drug dealers, school staff, or neighborhood social workers.

When conducting surveys, scientific sampling methods must be used to ensure representativeness. A sample is a segment of a particular population that is representative of the whole. Such nonrepresentative sampling techniques as quota sampling and snowball sampling, however, may be more appropriate in some situations. In quota sampling, the interviewer is assigned quotas for interviewing numbers of respondents but is not assigned specific individuals to interview. In snowball sampling, respondents refer the interviewer to other potential respondents.

Community Meetings. Program planners may establish goals and priorities at community meetings in which local residents state their opinions and give feedback. These meetings also help the program planner establish goals and priorities and add valuable insights into the nature of the problems.

The program planner must keep in mind, however, that participants at such meetings do not necessarily represent all community residents (i.e., are not a representative sample); they may, for example, overrepresent educated and/or politically active segments of the community.

Observational Methods. Checklists and protocols, as well as video and tape recorders, are used to document behaviors that relate to substance use. One problem with direct observation is that the presence of the observers may affect the behavior of the target group. On the other hand, observers who do not interrupt the natural events of the target audiences are often hampered by a greater distance from the behavior under investigation and a consequently greater reliance on inference that the behavior has occurred (Webb, Campbell, Schwartz, & Sechrest, 1966). For instance, schoolwide norms regarding cigarette smoking could be measured by observing the number of students who smoke, but it is likely that direct observation of this behavior would be obtrusive and discourage some students from smoking openly. Unobtrusive measures for this purpose may include counting the number of cigarette butts in student bathrooms.

Ethnographic Approaches. Here, participants are interviewed and observed in order to understand their cultural milieu. For a description of ethnographic methods for program evaluation, see Fetterman (1984, 1986), Fetterman and Pitman (1984), and Williams (1986).

Physiological Methods. Evans' development of the "bogus pipeline" technique (see Chapter 3) was a landmark for the incorporation of physiological measures in evaluating adolescent substance use.

Several physiological measures of alcohol ingestion are described by Leigh and Skinner (1988), including blood-alcohol concentration as measured by a breathalyzer, urine alcohol concentration as measured by a dipstick (also used for blood), and the sweat-patch. These methods record only transient volumes of alcohol; breath and urine tests are only relevant to drinking within the past 24 hours. Several laboratory tests have been devised to measure longer-term alcohol ingestion; these include gamma-glutamyl transferase GGT and mean corpuscular volume. HDL and GDH glutamate dehydrogenase levels are also tested for this purpose.

Since the pattern of substance use among youth may be one of intermittent episodes of acute, rather than chronic, substance use, laboratory tests for biochemical verification must be highly sensitive and specific. The test also must be administered regularly in order to measure both frequency and quantity of substance use. For these reasons, physiological testing is often impractical. Biochemical verification is employed most frequently to measure tobacco use in adolescents. Perhaps this restricted use is due to the difficulties of obtaining samples of bodily fluids for testing the presence of drugs, as compared to the ease of testing expired alveolar air or saliva for the presence of carbon monoxide or thiocyanate.

Financial Analysis. Detailed cost data are essential for cost-effectiveness or cost-benefit studies. Participant-program provider ratios per unit cost of materials and training time may be calculated and compared using financial records. Cost-benefit and cost-effectiveness analyses are used infrequently in program evaluation (Levin, 1987).

INSTRUMENTS FOR EVALUATION

The following section briefly describes some of the measures and indicators used in process, outcome, and impact evaluations of substance-use prevention programs. Three categories of measures are presented within each evaluation category: psychosocial, behavioral, and physiological.

Process-Evaluation Measures

Psychosocial Measures. These measures concern participant attitudes, values, beliefs, and knowledge about substances and their effects. The Situational Confidence Questionnaire—a self-report instrument measuring self-efficacy for alcohol-related situations—is an example of an evaluation using psychosocial measures (Annis & Davis, 1988). An important use of psychosocial variables would be to measure the beliefs of program staff that may influence program functioning.

Behavioral Measures. Behavioral indices directly related to process evaluation range in complexity from keeping attendance records to observing and analyzing social interactions. Self-report is probably the most efficient method of determining substance-use behaviors. Behavioral measures of greatest interest include amount, frequency, onset, and past cessation attempts.

Physiological Measures. Physiological measures are rarely used for process-evaluation purposes in prevention research, though they may be employed as process measures in prevention-outcome studies or in treatment studies.

Outcome-Evaluation Measures

Psychosocial Measures. Many prevention programs specify changes in participants' knowledge and understanding about substance use as an objective. Psychosocial measures to evaluate changes include knowledge concerning drugs and their effects, attitudes and beliefs concerning drug use, drug-related expectancies and values, knowledge of refusal and coping skills, and intentions related to substance use.

Psychosocial measures also may be used to evaluate perceptions of peers and their behaviors, perceived social support for abstaining from substance use, locus of control, environmental stress, self-esteem, and other intrapersonal variables (Schinke & Gilchrist, 1984b).

Behavioral Measures. Self-report is the method by which most prevention programs measure changes in substance use of study participants. Validity of self-reported substance use has been questioned, however, particularly for illicit substances. Methods for circumventing this problem include the use of consistency checks embedded within self-report instruments, for example, the inclusion of dummy drugs in a checklist; the use of weighted scoring, in which some substances are considered more serious than others; and the use of composite scoring, in which a single substance-use measurement is constructed from multiple measures of substance use.

Randomized response techniques (in which mathematical models are used to estimate responses to interview items) have been used to measure sensitive behaviors with greater accuracy (Fox & Tracy, 1986). Two important drawbacks of the randomized response technique are that only aggregate data are obtainable and that large sample sizes are required.

Behavior-rating scales may be completed by teachers, program staff, or clinicians. No matter which measurements are employed, it is essential to assure the study participant that confidentiality will not be breached. Program planners also must be wary of biases or influences. Instruments should be written in language that participants can understand and should be free of cultural, racial, gender, and sexual-orientation bias.

Physiological Measures. Many of the aforementioned physiological methods are appropriate for use in outcome studies. These tests are best suited for the validation of self-report of current substance use, because they usually measure transient or recent use. Such intermittent substance use as periodic episodes of heavy drinking or other substance use may not be detected, regardless of intensity. Physiological measures may not be used to reliably discriminate or categorize individuals as never-users, experimenters, quitters, or current users (Glynn, Leventhal, & Hirshman, 1985).

Impact Evaluation

Psychosocial Measures. Since impact evaluations examine generalized program effects throughout a community or organization, these effects may be measured or reported in aggregate or cumulative form (French & Kaufman, 1981) and do not require identification of respondents. Opinions, attitudes, beliefs, and knowledge are likely to be the variables in an impact evaluation of substance use.

Behavioral Measures. Large-scale behavioral effects are of greatest interest in an impact evaluation. Impact indicators of substance use include self-reported abstention or reduction in consumption; change in substance-use patterns; reduction in citations, arrests, or convictions for drug-related offenses; reduction in drug-related emergency-room incidents; fewer referrals to crisis or treatment centers; and decreased drug-related morbidity or mortality.

Physiological Measures. For reasons of cost and logistics, physiological measures are unlikely to be employed in impact evaluation.

RESEARCH DESIGN AND METHODOLOGICAL ISSUES

Campbell and Stanley's monograph (1963), which conceptualizes and presents various research designs, has received nearly universal acceptance by researchers in psychology and education. Their basic approach is to examine the strength of a research design against "common threats to valid inference." Campbell and Stanley distinguish between threats to internal validity, which obscure the true effect of the experimental intervention, and threats to external validity, which jeopardize the representativeness or generalizability of the study. Threats to validity that are most pertinent to substance-use prevention programs include the impact of historical events or trends; maturational or "developmental" processes operating over time, which may have contributed to or actually produced the apparent experimental effect; the effects of repeated testing; the statistical phenomenon of regression to the mean; selection biases or invalidity due to differential methods of recruiting members of treatment and control groups; attrition of study participants from treatment and control groups for different reasons or to varying degrees; and the interaction of two or more of these sources of invalidity (particularly selection bias with any other threats to validity).

The researcher must consider which validity threats may be operating in the planned intervention study and how their effects may be minimized. One of the central ideas espoused by Campbell and Stanley is the importance of randomly assigning study participants to treatment and comparison groups.

Table 5.1 presents a selection of research designs, with diagrams taken from Campbell and Stanley (1963). Threats to validity are noted for each design. Table 5.2, drawn from Flay (1985), describes selected first-through-fourth-generation adolescent smoking prevention programs, noting their research designs and some methodological problems.

Table 5.1 Internal Validity Strengths and Weaknesses to Five Evaluation Designs

				Threats to Internal Validity				
Design	History	Matu- ration	Testing	Instru- menta- tion	Regres- sion	Selec- tion	Attri- tion	Inter- active Effects
1. One group pretest and posttest E O X O	−	−	−	−	?	+	+	−
2. Nonequivalent control group E O X O C O O	+	+	+	+	?	+	+	−
3. Time series E OOO X OOO	−	+	+	?	+	+	+	+
4. Multiple time series E OOO X OOO C OOO OOO	+	+	+	+	+	+	+	
5. Pretest and posttest with control group R E O X O R C O O	+	+	+	+	+	−	?	?

SOURCE: T. D. Cook and D. T. Campbell, (1983). The design and conduct of quasi-experiments and true experiments in field settings. In M. D. Dunnette (Ed.), *Handbook of Industrial and Organizational Psychology.* (p. 00). New York: John Wiley. Reprinted by permission of the publisher.
NOTE: E = experimental group; C = control group; C = comparison group; O = observations; X = intervention; − = weakness; + = strength.

Methodological concerns and shortcomings of evaluations have been voiced many times. These concerns include nonrandom (biased) assignment to treatment conditions; preexisting differences between members of the treatment and control groups; excessive or differential attrition from the program; assigning intact units (e.g., classrooms or schools) to treatment groups but analyzing data as if individuals were randomly assigned to treatments; follow-up period of insufficient duration to detect long-term program effects; reliance on a single instrument, measure, or data-collection method; and insufficient numbers of study participants or units (e.g., treatment sites, communities).

Table 5.2 Research Designs and Threats to Validity Associated with Smoking Provision Studies from Generations 1 Through 4

Generation	Citation	Design Description	Threats to Validity
1	Evans et al., 1981	Nonequivalent control group	Group differences at pretest Attrition Reliance on cross-sectional analyses Analysis by individuals rather than school units
2	Botvin & Eng, 1980	Pretest-posttest control group design	Analysis by individuals rather than school units Brief follow-up (3 months) No biochemical validation of smoking status One school unit per condition
3	Arkin et al., 1981	Matched pairs Pretest-posttest with control group	Analysis by individuals rather than school units Pretest differences between groups Different treatment conditions not factorially organized Use of historical and non-equivalent control groups Serious attrition
4	Flay et al., 1989	Matched pairs Repeated measurements Pretest-posttest with control group	Pretest differences between groups Possible Hawthorne effect Possible measurement by treatment interaction

Recommendations

The following are issues and recommendations pertinent to the design and implementation of substance-use prevention program evaluations most frequently encountered in the literature:

(1) Maximize internal *and* external validity to the greatest possible extent.
(2) Block study units or respondents into different strata prior to randomization. Blocking reduces the proportion of unexplained variance, thereby enhancing statistical power and precision (Winer, 1971).

(3) Conduct construct-validity studies in such a manner that program components can be separately examined using process-evaluation procedures.

(4) Monitor the degree to which the program is faithfully implemented using process evaluation, and measure all factors that may affect outcomes, regardless of whether they are included in the program or intervention.

(5) Use passive consent procedures in which individuals are assumed to consent to their participation in the study if they or their parents do not actively refuse to participate. Passive consent procedures result in more representative samples of adolescents than do active consent procedures.

(6) Avoid an excessive reliance on a single data-collection method, particularly questionnaires.

(7) Use multiple measurements of critical variables.

(8) Work with individuals at high risk of substance use to establish that the program effects may be generalized to other, similar individuals or groups; low prevalence of substance use among low-risk groups may reduce statistical power to detect treatment effects.

(9) Use longitudinal designs that repeatedly measure the same study participants over a period of time to study long-term outcomes; repeated cross-sectional designs are likely to be confounded by individuals entering and leaving the group(s) being studied. Long-term effects on behavior must be demonstrated to validate claims of meaningful treatment effects.

(10) Minimize the negative effects of subject attrition by obtaining information about individuals who will likely know the whereabouts of dropouts from the study (Pirie et al., 1989).

(11) Optimize external, as well as internal, validity by examining study effects with different racial/ethnic, gender, and socioeconomic subgroups.

(12) Employ meta-analysis (secondary analysis of previously conducted research) to determine comparison standards for intervention efficacy.

(13) Calculate statistical power needs during the study design phase.

(14) Increase the number of measurement occasions to examine the longevity of intervention effects.

(15) Limit test obtrusiveness to minimize the likelihood that study participants will be affected by the repeated testing and the conspicuous attention paid to them (the Hawthorne effect).

(16) Design the study to include additional control groups, such as a group that receives only minimal substance-use treatment or general health-education advice.

(17) Attempt to replicate the intervention during the period of the study, perhaps using a research design in which different groups receive the programs at different times.

(18) Conduct large-scale multisite studies, including a diverse collection of schools, implementation measures, and outcome variables to optimize external validity.

(19) Combine process- and outcome-evaluation methods and measures (Judd, 1987; Judd & Kenny, 1981).

ANALYTIC ISSUES

Given the primary concern with establishing the validity of program effects, methodological, rather than analytic, concerns have been predominant in the field. In this section, we briefly describe some outstanding and some still unresolved data-analysis issues.

Multivariate Models

Dever, Rousseau, and Houser (1981) advocate a systems approach to evaluation that takes into account as many elements as possible, including health status, health resources, process of health programs, configuration of health systems, the effects of environment, and socioeconomic factors. To analyze such an intricate model requires the application of multivariate statistical techniques. Most often, related dependent variables are analyzed as if they were independent; that is, the variables are analyzed individually rather than jointly. An incongruity exists when models of substance use are based on the concept of interrelated behaviors (multivariate models) but analyzed using univariate statistical tools. We recommend the increased use of appropriate multivariate techniques in future evaluations.

Statistical Models of Causal Relationships

The literature concerning the analysis of causal relationships is large and growing. Bentler (1980) and researchers Zucker and Gomberg (1986) have begun to call for the use of statistical techniques to examine causal relations in the field of substance use. Bentler has pointed out that even if the observed data are compatible with a hypothesized model of causal relationships, it cannot be concluded that the statistical model mirrors the true causal process. Other causal models, as yet unspecified, also may be compatible with the observed data. Thus causal modeling cannot provide a definitive confirmation of underlying causal structure. A host of technical and mathematical issues require consideration prior to the use of these techniques; however, their further use in this field is highly recommended.

Analysis of Categorical Data

Due largely to the work of Goodman (1972), great advances have been made in the analysis of categorical outcome variables (such as smoker/nonsmoker). These new techniques, log-linear modeling of multi-way contingency tables and logistic regression methods, are now commonly used to analyze nominal variables, whether demographic variables (e.g., race, religion), independent variables (treatment condition), or outcomes. These statistical methods provide more opportunities for the analysis of complex data sets, but valid results still depend on such essential factors as appropriate research design, sufficient sample size, base rate of dependent variables, fidelity of treatment implementation, and magnitude of measurement error.

Analysis of Qualitative Data

It is important to distinguish between qualitative variables and qualitative methods. *Qualitative* apparently implies different things to different researchers (Guba, 1987) but is most frequently identified with the use of anthropological or ethnographic field methods for data collection and their presentation in "case studies." Until recently, few discussions of analytic methods for qualitative information were available. Miles and Huberman's sourcebook (1984) has become the reference in this area.

Survival Analysis Methods

Survival analysis is a statistical tool that has been used for the study of randomized controlled clinical trials (such as drug therapies) and, more recently, in outcome evaluation of substance-use prevention programs. The outcome of interest is the length of time until an event (e.g., cigarette smoking, drinking alcohol, or other substance use) occurs after an intervention (Brown & Peterson, 1989; Curry, Marlatt, Peterson, & Lutton, 1988; Greenhouse, Stangl, & Bromberg, 1989). One particular value of the survival-analysis technique is in the way that missing data are handled. When attrition rates may exceed 40% of study participants in a long-term outcome evaluation, study attrition is a serious practical problem (Hansen, Collins, Malotte, Johnson, & Fielding, 1985). Survival

analysis treats these data as censored observations that provide information pertinent to the estimation of treatment. Unlike other methods of
analysis, survival analysis uses data from all subjects, including incomplete data from individuals who drop out of the study before its final
measurement period.

Analyzing Data from Aggregate Units

In large-scale school-based adolescent substance-use prevention programs, assignment to condition is most often carried out at the school level
rather than at the individual level, but data from these study designs
frequently are analyzed as if individuals had been assigned to treatment
conditions. This method is used because there are generally insufficient
numbers of schools for statistical power to be great enough to detect
treatment effects. This method of analysis violates the assumption of
independent errors and creates possible systematic bias in the estimation
of treatment effects. Studies employing these designs should analyze data
at the level of assignment or use statistical methods that adjust for these
sources of error (Donner, 1985; Donner & Donald, 1987).

Meta-Analysis

The results of several meta-analyses of substance use prevention programs have been published (Bangert-Drowns, 1988; Rundall & Bruvold,
1988; Tobler, 1986), in addition to the numerous reviews of this literature.
In meta-analysis, a standardized unit of effect size is calculated, and
research findings are summarized using this common yardstick (Glass,
McGaw, & Smith, 1981). It should be pointed out, however, that (a) effect
sizes may be calculated in several ways; (b) variations in effect size may
not have clinical significance; (c) because meta-analysis is the analysis
of previously conducted research, the way in which studies are selected
for inclusion in the meta-analysis is extremely important, as are the
groupings or categories used in the meta-analysis; and (d) the quality of
the primary studies examined by the meta-analysis cannot be disregarded,
because the quality of the primary studies will, in part, affect the quality
and results of the meta-analysis.

Furthermore, meta-analytic conclusions may not agree. For example,
Bangert-Drowns (1988) found that no approach to substance-abuse education had any appreciable effects on substance-use behavior; Rundall
and Bruvold (1988) found that smoking interventions had moderate

success in altering longer-term (more than three months) smoking behavior; and Tobler (1986) found that peer programs maintained high effect size for reducing alcohol, soft drugs, and cigarette use.

SUMMARY

This chapter has examined a variety of measurement, design, and analytic issues relevant to the evaluation of substance-use prevention programs. The assumption of multiple and interacting causes in the determination of substance-use behaviors requires the application of multiple-domain (cigarette smoking, alcohol, and other substance use) and multiple-method (self-report, biochemical, and observational) measurement strategies, as well as multiple levels of analyses (individual, school, and community). Evaluation purposes and methods reflect the fact that program evaluation always is conducted in a political, as well as a scientific environment. A number of substance-use indicators were suggested, each of which may be more or less appropriate at different evaluation levels or phases. Validity—not only of experiments but also of treatment—remains a key issue in spite of advances in the methodological rigor of evaluation studies in the field. Some recommendations for improving validity were offered, and a number of promising analytic approaches were discussed.

6

THE DISSEMINATION OF INTERVENTIONS

INTRODUCTION

Researchers may successfully design, test, and evaluate a substance-abuse intervention, but these interventions are of no value if they do not impact and change substance-abuse behavior among individuals, groups, and society as a whole. In this chapter, we will look at the steps involved in going from the initial development of a substance-abuse intervention program to the achievement of a significant public health impact. The term *dissemination* has been used to define these steps.

DISSEMINATION SYSTEM

A dissemination system is the network of interrelationships between people and organizations that communicate new substance-abuse prevention information. Below we review the concept of a dissemination system in terms of three principal components: program effectiveness, program diffusion, and program implementation (see Figure 6.1).

A dissemination system is futile if interventions are not capable of bringing about their intended effects. This factor is termed *program effectiveness*. Moreover, interventions that are effective must also be accurately communicated and successfully adopted. These processes related to the communication and adoption of interventions are referred to as *program diffusion*. The former two components, though necessary, are not sufficient to ensure that programs will have any significant impact on public health. Effective interventions that have undergone diffusion and have been adopted in appropriate settings must also be consistently implemented and maintained over a sufficient period of time for intended

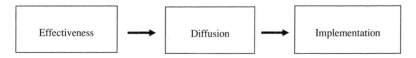

Figure 6.1. Three Components of Health-Promotion Dissemination Systems

effects to be realized. Therefore this third factor, *program implementation,* is critical to significant and sustained public-health impacts. Above, Figure 6.1 presents three components of health promotion dissemination systems.

PROGRAM EFFECTIVENESS

New interventions designed to influence health-related behavior are often referred to as *innovations* (Kolbe & Gilbert, 1984; Kolbe & Iverson, 1981). Substance-abuse prevention innovations have been developed in a variety of ways and, as a result, differ in several important respects. One important dimension that distinguishes different innovations is the degree to which evaluation is relied on as an integral developmental component (Kolbe & Gilbert, 1984).

One method of program development, for example, relies almost exclusively on personal and peer experiences rather than on tested research studies. This type of program development traditionally has taken place within such service-delivery settings as state and local departments of health, private and public school systems, and youth organizations. Understandably, in these settings there is an effort made to address high-priority problems rather than evaluation research (Orlandi, 1985).

When substance-abuse prevention programs are initiated through evaluation research, the orientation is considerably different. Research-based interventions are interested in determining if observed effects are, in fact, caused by the innovation or are merely coincidental. Usually, those who are more directly involved with controlling substance abuse are less concerned in identifying, in a scientifically rigorous manner, exactly how they have done so.

Five Phases of Innovation-Development Research

The U.S. Department of Health and Human Services (1987) has developed a paradigm that addresses research questions in a logical sequence.

The first phase of this process is *hypothesis development*. At this phase, broad conceptualizations are refined into specific hypotheses. *Applied research and methods development,* the second phase, involves the attempt to translate these hypotheses into testable intervention protocols, materials, and methods. The third phase, *efficacy testing,* follows as a series of smaller-scale studies with emphasis on internal, rather than external, validity. The aim at this point is to determine whether the innovation under development is feasible and capable of bringing about its intended result in a carefully controlled setting. Next, the innovation may be evaluated in larger-scale *clinical trials* to determine its effectiveness in a research sample drawn from larger groups. The emphasis in this fourth phase is on evaluating external validity in a larger, more heterogeneous population.

These four initial research phases lead to the last phase in the process, *demonstration and education research* in defined populations. At this point in the innovation-development process, the primary concerns are evaluating the barriers to successful dissemination and implementation.

Although this five-phase process seems categorically and fundamentally different from programs in a nonresearch environment, it actually is quite similar, with the only important difference being the degree of uncertainty that is tolerated before moving into more advanced stages of program implementation.

Limitations of This Paradigm. Despite the value that has been placed on this paradigm (Parcel, 1984), there is little evidence that innovations resulting from this process are necessarily more successful or more often put into application than those that do not (Iverson & Kolbe, 1983; Kolbe & Iverson, 1981).

A number of factors contribute to this inconsistency. First, individuals, groups, and organizations are often unaware of other research and evaluations that have been or are being done on substance-abuse prevention. Second, such research efforts as those supported by the National Institutes of Health typically are carried out among population subgroups that are easier to recruit and easier to follow up over time. Consequently, high-risk, high-need, hard-to-reach populations typically are excluded or underrepresented in such research programs. This lack often leads to the mistaken belief that the substance-abuse interventions developed through such research programs are appropriate for some population subgroups but are inappropriate and therefore irrelevant for others (Orlandi, 1986a). Third, serious challenges that are a normal and uncontrollable part of health promotion in the real world are often controlled in research studies and not taken into consideration during the early phases of the research process. For example, participants may be awarded a small stipend for their participation in a research project—a situation that is not likely to be replicated in a more typical substance-abuse intervention setting. Finally, since the focus of this research process is on shorter-term intervention effects, such longer-term issues as program diffusion, adoption, and maintenance are not often considered while the program is under development.

Even interventions that have evolved through the various stages of program development and evaluation may nonetheless fail to produce any meaningful public-health impact. One strategy for understanding and improving an intervention's potential for overall program impact is to analyze the way in which relevant research questions are addressed. The research process in its strictest form (as described above) is conceptualized as a series of sequential steps. The steps typically are described and carried out in a linear sequence. According to this approach, it is necessary to determine if an intervention is capable of bringing about an effect in a highly controlled research setting *before* exploring ways to make it applicable for the general population. While this fairly typical practice may result in intervention programs that are initially effective, it may possess a built-in potential for long-term overall dissemination failure (Orlandi, Landers, Weston, & Haley, in press). By addressing issues related to generalizability, acceptability, and diffusion as secondary rather than primary concerns, critical flaws that cannot easily be rectified by program repackaging may become incorporated into an intervention. In order to understand why this is the case and how this practice may be rectified, we must turn our attention now to the issues of program diffusion and adoption.

PROGRAM DIFFUSION

The next important step in the dissemination system is program diffusion. Too often, intervention programs are developed successfully but never delivered to the intended audiences. This section will discuss various aspects of diffusion theory that are directly related to substance-abuse prevention. But first, we will examine traditional concepts of diffusion.

Traditional Diffusion Theory

As stated earlier, new ideas, practices, informational technologies, or services are often referred to as *innovations,* and the process by which innovations are communicated from those who know and understand them to those who do not has been termed *diffusion.* Diffusion theory developed as an attempt to explain this communication process in a scientifically rigorous manner (Rogers, 1983).

The traditional approach to diffusion was to determine the most effective way to transfer to the real world what was learned in test settings. Underlying the early work in this area was the premise that the diffusion and adoption of an innovation was determined primarily by measurable scientific attributes and the needs of the adopter. This line of reasoning led to the assumption that if a particular innovation and the adopting organization were analyzed thoroughly, formulas for successful diffusion would result that could be applied to other innovations in other settings (U.S. Office of Technology Assessment, 1982).

Researchers have identified a number of attributes of successful diffusion effort (Kolbe & Iverson, 1981). These include the following.

Compatibility. Adoption is more likely to take place when innovations are consistent with the sociocultural, economic, and ideological value system of the adopter.

Flexibility. Innovations made up of components that can be applied separately will be applicable in a wider variety of settings.

Reversibility. Innovations that may be discontinued easily if the adopting individual or organization for any reason decided to revert to its previous practices are more likely to be adopted.

Relative Advantage. Innovations that appear to be beneficial when compared with current and previously used approaches or technologies are more likely to be adopted.

Complexity. Innovations that are difficult to grasp, either in theory or in practice, are less likely to be adopted.

Cost-Efficiency. Both the concrete and the abstract benefits of an innovation must outweigh its perceived costs if it is to be viewed as desirable.

Risk. Individuals and organizations vary greatly with respect to the amount of risk they are willing to accept, but, in general, innovations that entail considerable risk are more likely to be avoided.

Resource and User Systems. Innovations may be viewed as originating from a *resource system,* which has the knowledge and expertise required to generate innovative concepts. Concerning substance-abuse prevention innovations, the resource system includes all service providers and organizations, researchers, program developers, and other health professionals; health-education materials; and other written or otherwise documented information about approaches that have been successful.

The *user system* for substance abuse-prevention programs, broadly defined, includes health departments, schools, service organizations, youth organizations, and families, and, within these groupings, a variety of individuals including decision makers, administrators, teachers, counselors, other service providers, parents, and, ultimately, target children and adolescents.

Limitations of the Traditional Diffusion Model. Though the traditional diffusion model has contributed greatly to our general understanding of this important research area, it has been updated and refined in a number of significant ways (Basch, Eveland, & Portnoy, 1986; Rogers, 1983). First, the traditional approach focuses inappropriate attention on the characteristics of the user system (Greer, 1971; Russell, 1979). This one-sided focus fails to take into account the communication and transactional process that must take place between the resource and the user systems in order for an innovation to be adopted. Furthermore, this perspective has ignored the potential utility of innovation refinement and modification, both during and after innovation development.

Second, this orientation does not provide an adequate means of evaluating the potential contributions of efforts by the resource system or the user system to influence the diffusion process. In this sense, the process is viewed generally as static, rather than dynamic. Such contributions may include efforts to introduce the innovation in selected parts rather than as an unchangeable whole, to configure it differently, or to deliver it in ways that improve the likelihood of adoption so long as intervention integrity is still maintained.

Finally, the traditional model fails to recognize that the adoption decision is only one step in a multistep process.

Contemporary Perspectives

As noted above, a dissemination system for substance-abuse prevention innovations should be viewed as a communication process made up of interrelated steps. Recently, these steps have been redefined to identify five system-failure points, or critical barriers, that must be overcome in order for the overall system to achieve a lasting and meaningful impact (Basch, 1984; Orlandi et al., in press). These potential system-failure points include:

- *Innovation Failure.* The overall dissemination system may fail if it is inappropriately designed, inadequately evaluated, or improperly matched to the needs and sociocultural attributes of the target user population.

- *Communication Failure.* An innovation may be genuinely efficacious and have the potential to achieve its intended effect within the intended target group, yet fail to do so because it was communicated improperly. Failure at this stage may mean that the target user system was improperly informed about its availability or applicability or that inappropriate role models, symbolism, language, sources of information, etc., were employed (Orlandi, 1986b).

- *Adoption Failure.* Though fundamentally efficacious and properly communicated, an intervention may not be adopted due to a host of other factors ranging from differing value and belief systems to a lack of necessary funds or other resources.

- *Implementation Failure.* Despite being efficacious, well-communicated, and successfully adopted, an innovation may not be implemented properly or even at all. This frequently occurs when specific program components instrumental to the program's efficacy, such as instructor training, are omitted or drastically abbreviated. This is more likely to occur when programs are adopted at the organizational level (e.g., the corporation, clinic, school) and then implemented by the organization among its members (Orlandi, 1986b; Orlandi, 1987).

- *Maintenance Failure.* Even though a program may be successfully communicated, adopted, and initially implemented, it may lose its momentum easily and dissipate rapidly over time.

PROGRAM IMPLEMENTATION

As mentioned above, programs that are effective and have undergone successful diffusion and adoption still may fail to have any significant public-health impact if they are implemented inappropriately. To understand adequately the attributes of dissemination systems that succeed as well as those that fail, it is important to keep in mind that innovation success neither begins nor ends with the adoption decision. The next section of this chapter deals with factors related to implementation success and failure.

Program implementation refers to the way programs are carried out over a period of time. For successful implementation, certain barriers must be overcome. The fact that many barriers frequently are left unaddressed is evidenced by the number of substance-abuse prevention innovations that remain "on the shelf" after considerable developmental effort (Iverson & Kolbe, 1983; Kolbe & Iverson, 1981).

Why dissemination systems fail or succeed during implementation has not been evaluated adequately. As discussed in Chapter 4, any construct with multiple determinants must be considered in terms of interrelationships. Too often, program planners fail to take into account such factors as the idiosyncracies of the target group, special training needs, or unanticipated sociocultural incompatibility. Listed below are a number of common barriers or program-implementation issues relevant to the dissemination of substance-abuse prevention innovations (Kolbe & Gilbert, 1984).

- Lack of awareness regarding the potential uses of program-evaluation data and the ways in which these data may be used for program planning.
- Lack of understanding regarding the importance of maintaining intervention integrity as outlined in original protocols.
- Modifications of the intervention by program deliverers, administrators, and secondary trainers.
- Lack of training for program deliverers, administrators, and secondary trainers.
- Lack of priorities resulting from staff and administration turnover.
- Lack of involvement by educational agencies in health-promotion service-delivery activities.
- Lack of coordination among federal, state, and local departments of education and health.

- Lack of accepted measurement instruments to evaluate program outcomes.
- Lack of resources to maintain implementation efficacy adequately over time.

The effectiveness of a substance-abuse prevention intervention in one setting does not guarantee it will be effective in others settings. The dissemination process for substance-abuse prevention intervention is qualitatively different from that for an innovation like penicillin, which is meant to be delivered identically in every user setting. Medical innovations and other hard technologies require far less refinement and modification of the innovation to meet the specialized requirements of particular user settings (Cahill & Beljan, 1963; U.S. Office of Technology Assessment, 1982).

Linkage Approach

A methodology known as *linkage approach* is available to enhance the development, diffusion, and the implementation processes. This perspective was first described by Havelock (1969) and later expanded by others (Kolbe & Iverson, 1981; Orlandi, 1986b; Orlandi, 1987), and it involves the integration of these systems into a single general systems model (see Figure 6.2).

In addition to the resource and user subsystems already described, there are linkage subsystems. Linkage subsystems represent the exchanges and interactions that take place during innovation development, diffusion, and implementation. The individuals who interact within the linkage subsystem include representatives of the user system, the resource system, and *change agents*. The change agent's role is to facilitate collaboration objectively. A change agent may be an independent third party or members from the user or resource system. This collaborative process is intended to provide a mechanism for increasing the involvement of user group members in innovation development, diffusion, and implementation. For example, collaborating with teachers and administrators throughout the planning process for school-based programs helps avoid potential barriers to successful implementation and diffusion.

For this approach to function optimally, a specific perspective that defines the information exchange within the linkage subsystem must be maintained. This perspective is called *social marketing* (Bloom & Novelli, 1981; U.S. Department of Health, Education and Welfare, 1979). The initial role of the resource system, according to the social

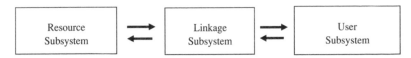

Figure 6.2. Communication Through a Linkage-Based Dissemination System

marketing perspective, is to help the user system determine its limitations, needs, and expectations and to make the user system aware of relevant innovations.

The techniques of social marketing research include a variety of methods for gathering relevant quantitative and qualitative data, addressing such issues as user group preferences, limitations, and perceived needs. The two key concepts directing these research activities are *segmentation* of a general population into relevant subgroups and *tailoring* an innovation to the particular characteristics of the targeted segments (Basch et al., 1986; Orlandi et al., in press) In this context, segmentation involves the identification of the various racial, ethnic, and sociocultural components that comprise the general target population. The tailoring process then follows in an attempt to improve the relevance and efficacy of a proposed social innovation with respect to these population components.

CONCLUSION

This chapter describes a rubric for substance-abuse prevention dissemination systems in terms of three principal program components: effectiveness, diffusion, and implementation. If substance-abuse prevention innovations are to have any significant impact on society as a whole, each of these components must be taken into consideration at every step of the program-development and service-delivery process.

Program-Effectiveness Issues

Since substance-abuse prevention programs have been developed in various settings and by interest groups with differing backgrounds and agendas, there would be considerable value in finding ways to improve the communication between groups developing interventions. In particular, communication must be strengthened between those in research settings and those in the field. One significant challenge in this area is to develop methods for transferring intervention programs aimed at narrowly defined target groups to broader segments of the population.

Program-Diffusion Issues

An innovation must be perceived as a significant improvement over whatever is in use. What has yet to be developed in the area of substance-abuse prevention is a set of accepted criteria for rating innovations. This lack of consensus remains the primary barrier to the diffusion of substance-abuse prevention innovations.

Research-oriented program developers, for example, place great stock in programs that are effective in carefully controlled experimental studies; service-oriented program developers are often more influenced by intervention approaches with proven durability through years of service in comparable settings. Few, if any, programs completely fulfill both criteria. Therefore, an urgent need exists to improve communications between the various resource and user system members and to underscore that they all are working on different aspects of the same problem. Creating more and better opportunities for collaboration between these different interest groups remains an important challenge for the future development of substance-abuse prevention programs.

Program-Implementation Issues

One principal barrier to achieving optimal program implementation and maintenance is that no one has been able to solve completely the training conundrum. Nearly everyone agrees that training is an important aspect of the delivery of substance-abuse prevention service, but beyond that, there is little on which general agreement exists. Some feel that without highly standardized training, maintaining intervention integrity is nearly impossible. Others disagree, asserting that individuals should seek training only to the extent that they feel they need it. Still, others consider this point moot, since lack of resources and an overburdened staff make taking any time away from service delivery an unaffordable luxury. Since maintaining intervention integrity is essential to achieving long-term program goals, creating strategies for ongoing training and for monitoring program implementation is a prerequisite for future development of substance-abuse prevention dissemination systems.

We must not only identify potential barriers to successful dissemination of effective intervention models but also overcome methodological flaws and inadequacies in research settings, and design programs that encompass a wide range of psychosocial factors.

Currently, empirically rigorous studies provide a compelling argument that prevention does, in fact, work. Still, more research is needed to refine these approaches further, to test their applicability to diverse populations, to examine issues related to implementation fidelity and provider training, and either to demonstrate long-term effects or determine the type of modifications necessary to sustain these effects over time.

REFERENCES

Allison, M., & Hubbard, R. L. (1985). Drug abuse treatment process: A review of the literature. *The International Journal of Addictions, 20*(9), 1321-1345.

Alwine, G. (1974). If you need love, come to US—an overview of a peer counseling program in a senior high school. *Journal of School Health, 44*, 463-464.

Annis, H. M., & Davis, C. S. (1988). Assessment of expectancies. In D. M. Donovan & G. A. Marlatt (Eds.), *Assessment of addictive behaviors.* New York: Guilford Press.

Arkin, R. M., Roemhild, H. J., Johnson, C. A., Luepker, R. V., & Murray, D. M. (1981). The Minnesota smoking prevention program: A seventh grade health curriculum supplement. *Journal of School Health, 51*, 616-661.

Associate Consultants (1981). *State of the art report on concerned parent groups.* Submitted to the National Institute on Drug Abuse.

Bailey, G. (1989). Current perspectives on substance abuse in youth. *Journal of the American Academy of Child Adolescent Psychiatry, 28*, 151-162.

Bandura, A. (1977). *Social learning theory.* Englewood Cliffs, NJ: Prentice-Hall.

Bangert-Drowns, R. L. (1988). The effects of school-based substance abuse education—a meta-analysis. *Journal of Drug Education, 18*, 243-264.

Basch, C. E. (1984). Research on disseminating and implementing health education programs in schools. *School Health Research, 54*, 57-66.

Basch, C. E., Eveland, J. D., & Portnoy, B. (1986). Diffusion systems for education and learning about health. *Family Community Health, 9*(2), 1-26.

Battjes, R. J. (1985). Prevention of adolescent drug abuse. *International Journal of Addictions, 20*(6,7), 1113-1134.

Becker, H. S. (1967). History, culture, and subjective experiences: An exploration of the social basis of drug induced experiences. *Journal of Health and Social Behavior, 8*, 163-176.

Bentler, P. M. (1980). Multivariate analysis with latent variables: Causal modeling. *Annual Review of Psychology, 31*, 419-456.

Berberian, R. M., Gross, C., Lovejoy, J., & Paparella, S. (1976). The effectiveness of drug education programs: A critical review. *Health Education Monographs, 4*, 377-398.

Best, J. A., Flay, B. R., Towson, S. M. J., Ryan, L. B., Perry, C., Brown, K. S., Kersell, M. W., & d'Avernas, J. R. (1984). Smoking prevention and the concept of risk. *Journal of Applied Social Psychology, 14*, 257-273.

Biglan, A., & Ary, D. V. (1985). Current methodological issues in research on smoking prevention. In C. Bell & R. Battjes (Eds.), *Prevention research: Deterring drug abuse among children and adolescents.* NIDA Research Monograph. Washington, DC: Government Printing Office.

Bloom, P. N., & Novelli, W. D. (1981). Problems and challenges in social marketing. *Journal of Marketing, 45*, 79-88.

Blum, R., & Richards, L. (1979). Youthful drug use. In R. I. Dupont, A. Goldstein, & J. O'Donnell (Eds.), *Handbook on drug abuse* (pp. 257-267). National Institute on Drug Abuse. Washington, DC: Government Printing Office.

Botvin, G. J. (1982). Broadening the focus of smoking prevention strategies. In T. Coates, A. Petersen, & C. Perry (Eds.), *Promoting adolescent health: A dialogue on research and practice*. New York: Academic Press.

Botvin, G. J. (1984). *Advances in substance abuse prevention*. The National Institute on Drug Abuse, First Triennial Report on Drug Abuse to the U.S. Congress. Washington, DC: Government Printing Office.

Botvin, G. J. (1986). Substance abuse prevention research: Recent developments and future directions. *Journal of School Health, 56*, 369-386.

Botvin, G. J., Baker, E., Botvin, E. M., Filazzola, A. D., & Millman, R. B. (1984). Alcohol abuse prevention through the development of personal and social competence: A pilot study. *Journal of Studies on Alcohol, 45*, 550-552.

Botvin, G. J., Baker, E., Filazzola, A., Botvin, E., Danilo, M., & Dusenbury, L. (1985). *A cognitive-behavioral approach into substance abuse prevention: A one year follow-up*. Paper presented at the 93rd annual meeting of the American Psychological Association, Los Angeles, CA.

Botvin, G. J., Baker, E., Renick, N., Filazzola, A. D., & Botvin, E. M. (1984). A cognitive-behavioral approach to substance abuse prevention. *Addictive Behaviors, 9*, 137-147.

Botvin, G. J., Dusenbury, L., Baker, E., & James-Ortiz, S. (1989). A skills training approach to smoking prevention among Hispanic youth. *Journal of Behavioral Medicine, 12*(3), 279-296.

Botvin, G. J., & Eng, A. (1980). A comprehensive school-based smoking prevention program. *Journal of School Health, 50*, 209-213.

Botvin, G. J., & Eng, A. (1982). The efficacy of a multicomponent approach to the prevention of cigarette smoking. *Preventive Medicine, 11*, 199-211.

Botvin, G. J., Eng, A., & Williams, C. L. (1980). Preventing the onset of cigarette smoking through life skills training. *Preventive Medicine, 9*, 135-143.

Botvin, G. J., Renick, N., & Baker, E. (1983). The effects of scheduling format and booster sessions on a broad spectrum psychosocial approach to smoking prevention. *Journal of Behavioral Medicine, 6*, 359-379.

Bradburn, N. M., & Sudman, S. (1979). *Improving interview method and questionnaire design*. San Francisco: Jossey-Bass.

Braucht, G. N., Follingstadt, D., Brakash, D., & Berry, K. L. (1973). Drug education: A review of goals, approaches and effectiveness, and a paradigm for evaluation. *Quarterly Journal of Studies on Alcohol, 34*, 1279-1292.

Brown, K. S., & Peterson, A. V. (1989). Statistical methods for the analysis of longitudinal data from school-based smoking prevention studies. *Preventive Medicine, 18*, 290-303.

Cahill, N. & Beljan, J. (1963). Technology assessment: Differing perspectives. *Journal of the American Medical Association, 252*(23), 32-94.

Campbell, D. T. & Stanley, J. C. (1963). *Experimental and quasi-experimental designs for research*. Chicago: Rand McNally.

Chelimsky, E. (1987). The politics of program evaluation. In D. S. Cordray, H. S. Bloom, & R. J. Light (Eds.), *Evaluation practice in review, new directions for program evaluation*. San Francisco: Jossey-Bass.

Christiansen, B. A., Smith, G. T., Roehling, P. V., & Goldman, M. S. (1989). Using alcohol expectancies to predict adolescent drinking behavior after one year. *Journal of Consulting and Clinical Psychology, 57,* 93-99.

Costanzo P., & Shaw, M., (1966). Conformity as a function of age level. *Child Development, 37,* 967-975.

Curry, S., Marlatt, G. A., Peterson, A. V., Jr., & Lutton, J. (1988). Survival analysis and assessment of relapse rates. In D. M. Donovan & G. A. Marlatt (Eds.), *Assessment of addictive behaviors.* New York: Guilford Press.

Degnan, E. J. (1972). An exploration into the relationship between depression and positive attitude toward drugs in young adolescents and an evaluation of a drug education program. *Dissertation Abstracts, 32*(11-B), 6614-6615.

Demone, H. W. (1973). The nonuse and abuse of alcohol by the male adolescent. In M. Chafetz (Ed.), *Proceedings of the Second Annual Alcoholism Conference.* (DHEW Publication No. HSM 73-9083). Washington, DC: Government Printing Office.

Dever, G. E. A., Rousseau, R. H., & Houser, F. M. (1981). Disease patterns, epidemiology, and evaluation: An evolutionary perspective. In R. J. Wooldridge (Ed.), *Evaluation of complex systems, new directions for program evaluation.* San Francisco: Jossey-Bass.

Dillman, D. A. (1978). *Mail and telephone surveys: The total design method.* New York: Wiley-Interscience.

Donner, A. (1985). A regression approach to the analysis of data arising from cluster randomization. *International Journal of Epidemiology, 14*(2), 322-326.

Donner, A., & Donald, A. (1987). Analysis of data arising from a stratified design with the cluster as unit of randomization. *Statistics in Medicine, 6,* 43-52.

Dorn, N., & Thompson, A. (1976). Evaluation of drug education in the longer term is not an optional extra. *Community Health, 7,* 154-161.

Ellickson, P. L. & Bell, R. M. (1990). Drug prevention in junior high: A multi-site longitudinal test. *Science, 247,* 1299-1305.

Evans, R. I. (1976). Smoking in children: Developing a social psychological strategy of deterrence. *Preventive Medicine, 5,* 122-127.

Evans, R. I., Henderson, A. H., Hill, P. C., & Raines, B. E. (1979). Current psychological, social and educational programs in control and prevention of smoking: A critical methodological review. *Atherosclerosis Reviews, 6,* 203-245.

Evans, R. I., Rozelle, R. M., Maxwell, S. E., Raines, B. E., Dill, C. A., Guthrie, T. J., Henderson, A. H., & Hill, P. C. (1981). Social modeling films to deter smoking in adolescents: Results of a three-year field investigation. *Journal of Applied Social Psychology, 66,* 399-314.

Evans, R. I., Rozelle, R. M., Mittlemark, M. B., Hansen, W. B., Bane, A. L., & Havis, J. (1978). Deterring the onset of smoking in children: Knowledge of immediate physiological effects and coping with peer pressure, media pressure, and parent modeling. *Journal of Applied Social Psychology, 8,* 126-135.

Fetterman, D. M. (1984). *Ethnography in educational evaluation.* Beverly Hills: Sage.

Fetterman, D. M. (1986). Conceptual crossroads: Methods and ethics in ethnographic evaluation. In D. D. Williams (Ed.), *Directions in Program Evaluation.* Beverly Hills, CA: Sage.

Fetterman, D. M., & Pitman, M. A. (1984). *Ethnographic evaluation: Theory, practice, and politics.* Beverly Hills, CA: Sage.

Fishbein, M. (1977). *Consumer beliefs and behavior with respect to cigarette smoking: A critical analysis of the public literature.* Federal Trade Commission report to

Congress pursuant to the Public Health Cigarette Smoking Act of 1976. Washington, DC: Government Printing Office.

Fisher, D. A., Armstrong, B. K., & de Kler, N. H. (1983). *A randomized-controlled trial of education for prevention of smoking in 12-year-old children.* Paper presented at the Fifth World Conference on Smoking and Health. Winnipeg, Canada.

Flay, B. R. (1985a). Psychosocial approaches to smoking prevention: A review of findings. *Health Psychology, 4,* 449-488.

Flay, B. R. (1985b). What we know about the social influences approach to smoking prevention: Review and recommendations. In C. S. Bell & R. Battjes (Eds.), *Prevention Research: Deterring Drug Abuse Among Children.* (NIDA Research Monograph No. 63). Washington: Department of Health and Human Services.

Flay, B., & Sobel, J. (1983). The role of mass media in preventing adolescent substance abuse. In T. Glynn, C. Luekefeld, and J. Ludford (Eds.), *Preventing adolescent drug abuse: Intervention strategies.* National Institute on Drug Abuse Research Monograph, 47 (DHEW Pub. No. ADM83-1280). Washington, DC: Government Printing Office.

Flay, B. R., Koepke, D., Thomson, S. J., Santi, S., Best, J. A., & Brown, K. S. (1989). Six-year follow-up of the first Waterloo School smoking prevention trial. *American Journal of Public Health, 79*(10), 1371-1376.

Fox, J. A., & Tracy, P. E. (1986). *Randomized response techniques.* Beverly Hills, CA: Sage.

French. J. F., & Kaufman, N. J. (1981). *Handbook for prevention evaluation.* National Institute on Drug Abuse. Washington, DC: Government Printing Office.

Friedman, S. M. (1973). A drug education program emphasizing affective approaches and its influence upon intermediate school student and teacher attitudes. *Dissertation Abstracts, 34*(5-A), 2270.

Gerhard, R. J. (1981). The organizational imperative. In R. J. Wooldridge (Ed.), *Evaluation of complex systems, new directions for program evaluation.* San Francisco: Jossey-Bass.

Gilchrist, L. D., & Schinke, S. P. (1983). Self-control skills for smoking prevention. In P. F. Engstrom & P. Anderson (Eds.), *Advances in cancer control.* New York: Alan R. Liss.

Glasgow, R. E., & McCaul, K. D. (1985). Life skills training programs for smoking prevention: Critique and directions for future research. In C. Bell & R. Battjes (Eds.), *Prevention research: Deterring drug abuse among children and adolescents.* Washington, DC: Government Printing Office.

Glass, G. V., McGaw, B., & Smith, M. L. (1981). *Meta-analysis in social research.* Beverly Hills, CA: Sage.

Glynn, K., Leventhal, H., & Hirshman, R. (1985). A cognitive developmental approach to smoking prevention. In C. S. Bell & R. Battjes (Eds.), *Prevention research: Deterring drug abuse among children.* (NIDA Research Monograph No. 63). Washington: Department of Health and Human Services.

Goodman, L. A. (1972). A modified multiple regression approach to the analysis of dichotomous variables. *American Sociological Review, 37*(2), 28-46.

Goodstadt, M. S. (1974). Myths and methodology in drug education: A critical review of the research evidence. In M. S. Goodstadt, (Ed.), *Research on methods and programs of drug education.* Toronto: Addiction Research Foundation.

Green, L. W. (1985). *Toward a healthy community: Organizing events for community health promotion.* Washington, DC: Government Printing Office.

Greenhouse, J. B., Stangl, D., & Bromberg, J. (1989). An introduction to survival analysis: Statistical methods for analysis of clinical trial data. *Journal of Consulting and Clinical Psychology, 57,* 536-544.

Greer, A. L. (1971). Advances in the study of diffusion of innovations in health care organizations. *Milbank Memorial Fund Quarterly: Health and Society, 55,* 505-532.

Guba, E. G. (1987). Naturalistic evaluation. In D. S. Cordray, H. S. Bloom, & R. J. Light (Eds.), *Evaluation practice in review, new directions for program evaluation.* San Francisco: Jossey-Bass.

Hamburg, B. A., & Varenhorst, B. B. (1972). Peer counseling in the secondary schools: A community mental health project for youth. *American Journal of Orthopsychiatry, 42,* 566-581.

Hansen, W. B., Collins, L. M., Malotte, C. K., Johnson, C. A., & Fielding, J. E. (1985). Attrition in prevention research. *Journal of Behavioral Medicine, 8*(3), 261-275.

Hartup, W. (1970). Peer interaction and social organization. In P. Mussen (Ed.), *Carmichael's manual of child psychology.* New York: John Wiley.

Havelock, R. (1969). *Planning for innovation through dissemination and utilization of knowledge.* Ann Arbor: University of Michigan.

Hops, H., Weissman, W., Biglan, A., Thompson, R., Faller, C., & Severson, H. H. (in press). A taped situation test of cigarette refusal skill among adolescents. *Behavioral Assessment.*

Hurd, P., Johnson, C. A., Pechacek, T., Best, C. P., Jacobs, D., & Luepker, R. (1980). Prevention of cigarette smoking in 7th grade students. *Journal of Behavioral Medicine, 3,* 15-28.

Isralowitz, R., & Singer, M. (1983). *Adolescent substance abuse: A guide to prevention and treatment.* New York: Haworth Press.

Iverson, D., & Kolbe, L. (1983). Evolution of the national disease prevention and health promotion strategy: Establishing a role for the schools. *Journal of School Health, 5,* 294-302.

Jessor, R. (1976). Predicting time of onset of marijuana use: A developmental study of high school youth. In D. J. Lettieri, (Ed.), *Predicting adolescent drug abuse: A review of issues, methods and correlates.* Research Issues 11. (DHEW Publication No. ADM 77-299). Washington, DC: Government Printing Office.

Jessor, R. (1982). Critical issues in research on adolescent health promotion. In T. Coates, A. Petersen, & C. Perry (Eds.), *Promoting adolescent health: A dialogue on research and practice* (pp. 447-465). New York: Academic.

Jessor, R., Collins, M. I., & Jessor S. L. (1972). On becoming a drinker: Social-psychological aspects of adolescent transition. *Annual of the New York Academy of Sciences, 197,* 199-213.

Jessor, R., & Jessor, S. L. (1977). *Problem behavior and psychosocial development: A longitudinal study of youth.* New York: Academic.

Johnston, L. D., O'Malley, P. M., & Bachman, J. G. (1989). *Drug use, drinking, and smoking: National survey results from high school, college, and young adults populations 1975-1988.* National Institute on Drug Abuse. Washington, DC: Government Printing Office.

Judd, C. M. (1987). Combining process and outcome evaluation. In M. M. Mark & R. L. Shotland (Eds.), *Multiple methods in program evaluation.* San Francisco: Jossey-Bass.

Judd, C. G., & Kenny, D. A. (1981). Process analysis: Estimating mediation in treatment evaluations. *Evaluation review, 5,* 602-619.

Kearney, A. L., & Hines, M. H. (1980). Evaluation of the effectiveness of a drug prevention education program. *Journal of Drug Education, 10,* 127-134.

Kim, S. (1988). *A short- and long-term evaluation of Here's Looking at You alcohol education program.* Paper submitted for publication.

Kinder, B., Pape, N., & Walfish, S. (1980). Drug and alcohol education programs: A review of outcome studies. *The International Journal of the Addictions, 15,* 1035-1054.

Kolbe, L. J., & Gilbert, G. G. (1984). Involving the schools in the international strategy to improve the health of Americans. *Proceedings of Prospects For a Healthier America: Achieving the Nation's Health Promotion Objectives* (pp. 63-66). Office of Disease Prevention and Health Promotion: U.S. Department of Health and Human Services.

Kolbe, L. J., & Iverson, D. C. (1981). Implementing comprehensive health education: Educational innovations and social change. *Health Education Quarterly, 8*(1), 57-80.

Leigh, G., & Skinner, H. A. (1988). Physiological assessment. In D. M. Donovan & G. A. Marlatt (Eds.), *Assessment of addictive behaviors.* New York: Guilford Press.

Levin, H. M. (1987). Cost-benefit and cost-effectiveness analyses. In D. S. Cordray, H. S. Bloom, & R. J. Light (Eds.), *Evaluation practice in review, new directions for program evaluation.* San Francisco: Jossey-Bass.

Luepker, R. V., Johnson, C. A., Murray, D. M., & Pechacek, T. F. (1983). Prevention of cigarette smoking: Three year follow-up of educational programs for youth. *Journal of Behavioral Medicine, 6,* 53-61.

Maccoby, E., & Masters, J. (1970). Attachment and dependency. In P. H. Mussen, (Ed.), *Carmichael's manual of child psychology,* (3rd ed., Vol. 2). New York: John Wiley.

MacDonald, D. I. (1984). *Drugs, drinking and adolescents.* Chicago: Year Book Medical Publishers.

Malvin, J., Moskowitz, J., Schaps, E., & Schaeffer, G. (1985). Evaluation of two school-based alternatives programs. *Journal of Alcohol Drug Education, 30,* 98-108.

Manett, M. (1983). *Parents, peers and pot II: Parents in action.* (DHHS Publication No. ADM 83-1290). Washington, DC: Government Printing Office.

Mason, M. L. (1973). Drug education effects. *Dissertation Abstracts, 34*(4-B), 418.

McAlister, A., Perry, C. L., Killen, J., Slinkard, L. A., & Maccoby, N. (1980). Pilot study of smoking, alcohol, and drug abuse prevention. *American Journal of Public Health, 70,* 719-721.

McAlister, A., Perry, C., & Maccoby, N. (1979). Adolescent smoking: Onset and prevention. *Pediatrics, 63,* 650-658.

McGuire, W. J. (1964). Inducing resistance to persuasion: Some contemporary approaches. In L. Berkowitz (Ed.), *Advances in experimental social psychology* (Vol. 1, pp. 192-227). New York: Academic Press.

McGuire, W. J. (1968). The nature of attitudes and attitude change. In B. Lindzey & E. Aronson (Eds.), *Handbook of social psychology* (pp. 136-314). Reading, MA: Addison-Wesley.

McLellan, A. T., Luborsky, L., O'Brien, C. P., Woody, G. E., & Druley, K. A. (1982). Is treatment for substance abuse effective? *Journal of the American Medical Association, 247,* 1423-1428.

McRae, C. F., & Nelson, D. M. (1971). Youth to youth communication on smoking and health. *Journal of School Health, 41,* 445-447.

Meyer, R. E., & Mirin, S. M. (1979). *The heroin stimulus: Implications for a theory of addiction.* New York and London: Plenum Medical Book Co.

Miles, M. B., & Huberman, A. M. (1984). *Qualitative data analysis: A sourcebook of new methods.* Beverly Hills, CA: Sage.

Millman, R. B., & Botvin, G. J. (1983). Substance use, abuse, and dependence. In M. D. Levine, W. B. Carey, A. C. Crocker, & R. T. Gross (Eds.), *Developmental-behavioral pediatrics* (pp. 683-708). Philadelphia: W. B. Saunders.

Moberg, D. P. (1983). Identifying adolescents with alcohol problems: A field test of the adolescent alcohol involvement scale. *Journal of Studies on Alcohol, 44,* 701-722.

Moskowitz, J. M. (1985). Evaluating the effects of parent groups on the correlates of adolescents substance abuse. *Journal of Psychoactive Drugs, 17*(3), 173-178.

Moskowitz, J. M., Schaps, E., & Malvin, J. H. (1982). Process and outcome evaluation in a primary prevention: The Magic Circle program. *Evaluation Review, 6,* 775-788.

Moskowitz, J. M., Schaps, E., Malvin, J., & Schaeffer, G. (1985). The effects of drug education at follow-up. *Journal of Alcohol and Drug Education, 30,* 45-49.

Murray, D. M., Johnson, C. A., Luepker, R. V., Pechacek, T. F., & Jacobs, D. R. (1980). *Issues in smoking prevention research.* Paper presented at American Psychological Association, Montreal, Canada.

Mussen, P., Conger, J., & Kagan, J. (1974). *Child development and personality* (4th ed.). New York: Harper & Row.

Nunnally, J. (1978). *Psychometric theory.* (2nd ed.). New York: McGraw-Hill.

Orlandi, M. A. (1985). Strategic planning for school-based tobacco control initiatives: An analysis of opportunities and barriers. *Proceedings of the Pennsylvania Consensus Conference on Tobacco and Health Priorities.* Pennsylvania Department of Health.

Orlandi, M. A. (1986a). Community-based substance abuse prevention: A multicultural perspective. *Journal of School Health, 56*(9), 394-401.

Orlandi, M. A. (1986b). The diffusion and adoption of worksite health promotion innovations: An analysis of the barriers. *Preventive Medicine, 15*(3), 522-536.

Orlandi, M. A. (1987). Promoting health and preventing disease in health care settings: An analysis of barriers. *Preventive Medicine, 16,* 119-130.

Orlandi, M. A., Landers, C., Weston, R., & Haley, N. (in press). Diffusion of health promotion innovations. In Glanz, K., Lewis, F. M., Rimer, B. K. (Eds.), *Health behavior and health education: Theory, research and practice.* San Francisco: Jossey-Bass.

O'Rourke, T. W. & Barr, S. L. (1974). Assessment of the effectiveness of the New York state drug curriculum guide with respect to drug attitudes. *Journal of Drug Education. 4*(3), 347-356.

Parcel, G. (1984). Theoretical models for the application of school health education research. *Journal of School Health, 54,* 39-49.

Patton, M. Q. (1981) *Creative evaluation.* Beverly Hills, CA: Sage.

Pentz, M. A. (1983). Prevention of adolescent substance abuse through social skill development. In T. J. Glynn, C. G. Leukefeld, & J. P. Ludford (Eds.), *Preventing adolescent drug abuse: Intervention strategies* (pp. 195-232). (NIDA Research Monograph No. 47). Washington, DC: Government Printing Office.

Pentz, M. A. (1986). Community organization and school liaisons: How to get programs started. *Journal of Public Health, 56,* 9.

Pentz, M. A., Cormack, C., Flay, B., Hansen, W., & Johnson, C. A. (1986). Balancing program and research integrity in community drug abuse prevention: Project STAR approach. *Journal of School Health, 56* (9), 389-393.

Pentz, M. A., MacKinnon, D. P., Dwyer, J. H., Wang, E. Y., Hansen, W. B., Flay, B. R., & Johnson, C. A. (1989). Longitudinal effects of the midwestern prevention project on regular and experimental smoking in adolescents. *Preventive Medicine, 18,* 304-321.

Perry, C. L., Killen, J., Telch, M., Slinkard, L. A., & Danaher, B. G. (1980). Modifying smoking behavior of teenagers: A school-based intervention. *American Journal of Public Health, 70,* 772-725.

Perry, C., Killen, J., Slinkard, L. A., & McAlister, A. L. (1980). Peer teaching and smoking prevention among junior high students. *Adolescence, 9,* 277-281.

Perry, C. L., Klepp, K., Halper, A., Hawkins, K. G., & Murray, D. M. (1986). A process evaluation study of peer leaders in health education. *Journal of School Health, 56*(2), 62-67.

Perry, C. L., Telch, M. J., Killen, J., Dass, R., & Maccoby, N. (1983). High school smoking prevention: The relative efficacy of varied treatments and instructors. *Adolescence, 18,* 562-566.

Piaget, J. (1962). *The moral judgment of the child.* New York: Collier.

Pirie, P. L., Thomson, S. J., Mann, S. L., Peterson, A. V., Murray, D. M., Flay, B. R., & Best, J. A. (1989). Attrition in longitudinal school-based smoking prevention research. *Preventive Medicine, 18,* 249-257.

Ray, O. S. (1974). *Drugs, society, and human behavior.* St. Louis: C. V. Mosby.

Richards, L. G. (1969). *Government programs and psychological principals in drug abuse education.* Paper presented at annual convention of American Psychological Association. Washington, DC.

Richardson, D. W., Nader, P. R., Rochman, K. J., & Freidman, S. B. (1972). Attitudes of fifth grade students to illicit psychoactive drugs. *Journal of School Health, 42*(7), 389-391.

Rogers, E. M. (1983). *The diffusion of innovations.* New York: Macmillan.

Rosenblitt, D. L., & Nagey, D. A. (1973). The use of medical manpower in a seventh grade drug education program. *Journal of Drug Education, 3*(1), 39-56.

Rossi, P. H., & Freeman, H. E. (1985). *Evaluation: A systematic approach* (3rd ed.). Beverly Hills, CA: Sage.

Rothman, J., Erlich, J. L., & Teresa, J. G. (1981). *Changing organizations and community programs.* Beverly Hills, CA: Sage.

Rundall, T. G., & Bruvold, W. H. (1988). A meta-analysis of school-based smoking and alcohol use prevention programs. *Health Education Quarterly, 15*(3), 317-334.

Russell, L. B. (1979). *Technologies in hospitals: Medical advances and their diffusion.* Washington, DC: Brookings Institute.

Rutman, L. (1977). Planning an evaluation study. In L. Rutman (Ed.), Evaluation research methods: A basic guide. Beverly Hills, CA: Sage.

Schaps, E., Bartolo, R. D., Moskowitz, J., Palley, C. S., & Churgin, S. (1981). A review of 127 drug abuse prevention program evaluations. *Journal of Drug Issues, 12,* 17-43.

Schaps, E., Moskowitz, J., Condon, J., & Malvin, J. (1982). Process and outcome evaluation of a drug education course. *Journal of Drug Education, 12,* 253-364.

Schaps, E., Moskowitz, J. M., Malvin, J., & Schaeffer, G. (1983). *Napa project summary.* Unpublished report for Pacific Institute for Research and Evaluation. Lafayette, CA.

Schinke, S. P. (1984). Preventing teenage pregnancy. In M. Hersen, R. M. Eisler, & P. M. Miller (Eds.), *Progress in behavior modification* (Vol. 16, pp. 31-63). New York: Academic.

Schinke, S. P., & Blythe, B. J. (1981). Cognitive-behavioral prevention of children's smoking. *Child Behavior Therapy, 3*, 25-42.

Schinke, S. P., & Gilchrist, L. D. (1983). Primary prevention of tobacco smoking. *Journal of School Health, 53*(7), 416-419.

Schinke, S. P., & Gilchrist, L. D. (1984a). *Life skills counseling with adolescents.* Austin, TX: Pro-Ed.

Schinke, S. P., & Gilchrist, L. D. (1984b). Preventing cigarette smoking with youth. *Journal of Primary Prevention, 5,* 48-56.

Semlitz, L., & Gold, M. S. (1986). Adolescent drug abuse. *Psychiatric Clinics of North America, 9,* 455-473.

Stenmark, D., Kinder, B., & Milne, L. (1977). Drug-related attitudes and knowledge of pharmacy students and college undergraduates. *International Journal of Addictions, 12*(1), 153-160.

Swisher, J. D. (1979). Prevention issues. In R. I. Dupont, A. Goldstein, & J. O'Donnell (Eds.), *Handbook on drug abuse* (pp. 49-62). National Institute on Drug Abuse. Washington, DC: Government Printing Office.

Swisher, J. D., Crawford, J. L., Goldstein, R., & Yura, M. (1971). Drug education: Pushing or preventing? *Peabody Journal of Education, 49,* 68-75.

Swisher, J. D., & Hoffman, A. (1975). Information: The irrelevant variable in drug education. In B. W. Corder, R. A. Smith, and J. D. Swisher, (Eds.), *Drug abuse prevention: Perspectives and approaches for educators* (pp. 49-62). Dubuque, IA: William C. Brown.

Swisher, J. D., & Hu, T. W., (1983). Alternatives to drug abuse: Some are and some are not. In T. J. Glynn, C. G. Leukefeld, J. P. Ludford, (Eds.), *Preventing adolescent drug abuse: Intervention strategies.* U.S. Public Health Service, NIDA (DHHS Publication No. ADM 83-1280. Washington, DC: Government Printing Office.

Telch, M. J., Killen, J. D., McAlister, A. L., Perry, C. L., & Maccoby, N. (1982). Long-term follow-up of a pilot project on smoking prevention with adolescents. *Journal of Behavioral Medicine, 5,* 1-8.

Tobler, N. S. (1986). Meta-analysis of 143 adolescent drug prevention programs: Quantitative outcome results of program participants compared to a control or comparison group. *Journal of Drug Issues, 16*(4), 537-567.

U.S. Department of Health, Education and Welfare. (1979). *Healthy people: The Surgeon General's report on health promotion and disease prevention.* Washington, DC: Government Printing Office.

U.S. Department of Health and Human Services. (1979). *Multicultural perspectives on drug abuse and its prevention: A resource book.* National Institute on Drug Abuse. (DHHS Publication No. ADM 78-671). Washington, DC: Government Printing Office.

U.S. Department of Health and Human Services. (1987). *Guidelines for demonstration and education research grants.* (No. 61116, pp. 181-296). Washington, DC: Government Printing Office.

U.S. Office of Technology Assessment. (1982). *Technology transfer at the National Institutes of Health.* (DHHS Publication No. ADM 11-4822). Washington, DC: Government Printing Office.

U.S. Public Health Service. (1986). *Drug abuse and drug abuse research: The second triennial report to Congress from the Secretary.* (DHHS Publication No. ADM 87-1486). Washington, DC: Government Printing Office.

Utech, D., & Hoving, K. L. (1969). Parents and peers as competing influences in the decisions on children of differing ages. *Journal of Social Psychology, 78*, 267-274.

Vriend, T. (1969). High-performing inner-city adolescents assist low-performing peers in counseling groups. *Personnel Guidance Journal, 48*, 897-904.

Walters, R., Marshall, W., & Shooter, J. (1960). Anxiety, isolation, and susceptibility to social influence. *Journal of Personality, 28*, 518-529.

Warheit, G. J., Bell, R. A., & Schwab, J. J. (1977). *Needs assessment approaches: Concepts and methods.* Washington, DC: U.S. Department of Health, Education, and Welfare.

Watzlawick, F., Weakland, J. H., & Fisch, R. (1974). *Change: Principles of problem formation and problem resolution.* New York: Norton.

Webb, E. J., Campbell, D. T., Schwartz, R. D., & Sechrest, L. (1966). *Unobtrusive measures: Nonreactive research in the social sciences.* Chicago: Rand McNally.

Wechsler, H. (1976). Alcohol intoxication and drug use among teenagers. *Journal of Studies in Alcohol, 37*, 1672-1677.

Wechsler, H., & Thum, D. (1973). Alcohol and drug use among teenagers: A questionnaire study. In M. Chafetz (Ed.), *Proceedings of the Second Annual Alcoholism Conference* (pp. 33-46). (DHEW Publication No. HSM 73-9083). Washington, DC: Government Printing Office.

Weir, W. R. (1968). A program of alcohol education and counseling for high school students with and without a family alcohol problem. *Dissertation Abstracts, 28*(11-A), 4454-4455.

Weiss, C. H. (1983). The stakeholder approach to evaluation: Origins and promise. In A. S. Bryk (Ed.), *Stakeholder-based evaluation, new directions for program evaluation.* San Francisco: Jossey-Bass.

Wheeler, K., & Malmquist, J. (1987). Treatment approaches in adolescent chemical dependency. *Pediatric Clinics of North America, 34*(2), 437-447.

Wholey, J. S. (1977). Evaluability assessment. In L. Rutman (Ed.), *Evaluation research methods: A basic guide.* Beverly Hills, CA: Sage.

Williams, R. A., Feibelman, N. D., & Moulder, C. (1989). Events precipitating hospital treatment of adolescent drug abusers. *Journal of the American Academy of Child and Adolescent Psychiatry, 28*, 70-73.

Williams, D. D. (1986). *Naturalistic evaluation, new directions in program evaluation.* Beverly Hills, CA: Sage.

Windsor, R. A., Baranowski, T., Clark, N., & Cutter, G. (1984). *Evaluation of health promotion and education programs.* Palo Alto, CA: Mayfield.

Winer, B. J. (1971). *Statistical principles in experimental design.* New York: McGraw-Hill.

Winick, C., & Winick, M. P. (1976). Drug education and a content of mass media dealing with "dangerous drugs" and alcohol. In R. E. Osteman (Ed.), *Communication research and drug education* (Vol. 4). London: Sage.

Winters, K. C., & Henley, G. (1988). Assessing adolescents who abuse chemicals: The chemical dependency adolescent assessment project. In E. R. Rahdert & J. Grabowski (Eds.), *Adolescent drug abuse analyses of treatment research.* (NIDA Monograph No. 77). Rockville, MD: National Institute on Drug Abuse.

Wolf, F. M. (1986). *Meta-analysis: Quantitative methods for research synthesis.* Sage University Paper Series on Quantitative Applications in the Social Sciences, No. 59. Beverly Hills, CA: Sage.

Zucker, R. A., & Gomberg, E. S. L. (1986). Etiology of alcoholism reconsidered: The case for a biopsychosocial process. *American Psychologist, 41*, 783-793.

AUTHOR INDEX

SUBJECT INDEX

ABOUT THE AUTHORS

Steven P. Schinke, Ph.D., was trained in social welfare and research methodology at the University of Wisconsin, in Madison. Subsequently, he served on the faculty of the University of Washington, in Seattle. He is currently Professor at the Columbia University School of Social Work in New York City. At Columbia, he is involved in research on substance abuse in children and adolescents relative to the development and testing of interventions for African-American, Hispanic, Native American, and majority culture youth. He has also researched stress-management interventions among adolescents and the prevention of unplanned adolescent pregnancy. He presently serves as a consulting editor to *The Journal of Adolescent Research* and is on the editorial board of *The Journal of Family Violence and Addictive Behaviors.* He has published over 150 articles dealing with preventive interventions and skills training for adolescents and is coauthor (with L. D. Gilchrist) of *Life Skills Counseling with Adolescents.*

Gilbert J. Botvin, Ph.D., was trained in developmental and clinical psychology at Columbia University. He then spent three years at the American Health Foundation, first as a staff psychologist and later as director of child health behavior research. Currently, he is Associate Professor in the departments of public health and psychiatry and is the Director of the Laboratory of Health-Behavior Research at Cornell University Medical College. He holds an appointment at the New York Hospital-Cornell Medical Center as Associate Attending Psychologist where he treats substance-abuse patients. His research on the life skills training approach to problem behavior prevention and health promotion among adolescents represents the forefront of theory and empirical knowledge on interventions for youth.

Mario A. Orlandi, M.P.H., Ph.D., was trained in neurobiology, psychology, and public health at Duke University and Harvard University. After teaching at Harvard, he took the position of chief of the division of health promotion research at the American Health Foundation. He also holds an appointment at the Columbia University School of Social Work as an adjunct research scientist. He specializes in skills-development intervention research with youth at risk for health-behavior problems. Currently, he is the principal investigator and a coinvestigator of community-based studies on chronic disease reduction among adolescents and adults and on related preventive-intervention and health-promotion studies in New York and in the Southwestern United States. He has published work in *Drugs & Society, The Journal of the American Medical Association, Smoking and Health,* and *Preventive Medicine.*